AUCTIONEERS WHO MADE ART HISTORY

# AUCTIONEERS WHO MADE ART HISTORY

Edited by  DIRK BOLL

With texts by  URSULA BODE
DIRK BOLL
BARBARA BONGARTZ
THIS BRUNNER
WALTER FEILCHENFELDT
CELINA FOX
JAMES GOODWIN
ROSE-MARIA GROPP
ALBERT KRIEMLER
DANIELLA LUXEMBOURG
CHRISTOPHER MAXWELL
DAVID NASH
AMIE SIEGEL
STEPHANIE TASCH
JUDD TULLY
BRIGITTE ULMER
WOLFGANG WITTROCK

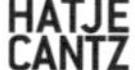
HATJE
CANTZ

DIRK BOLL

# A Cultural History of the Art Auction in 14 Portraits

It is possible that money has always played a role in the perception of art. Certainly this became obvious in the 1980s, when collectors from Japan bought Impressionist paintings following the investment of British pension funds in this category a few years earlier. Similarly, everybody began to buy Contemporary Art in the 1990s. These days it is an accepted fact that the market value of art has a bearing on the canonisation process. We may regret this, but it is unlikely to change any time soon. The all-encompassing transparency that the Internet now brings to the market practically guarantees a grassroots democratic approach and also leaves an indelible mark. Since more than half of all art works sold globally in 2013 achieved prices below €3,000, the market clearly also plays an important role in popularizing the arts.[1]

Even though art markets follow traditional rules and regulations, they have been subject to unprecedented change since the turn of the millennium. At last, auction houses have achieved a transformation from wholesaler to retail business. This was only possible once they had established themselves in the eyes of the buyer as a third channel of commerce alongside art fairs on the one hand and galleries and dealerships on the other. New auction buyers are mainly 'end consumers' who are willing to pay higher prices than traders and are receptive to client development activities.

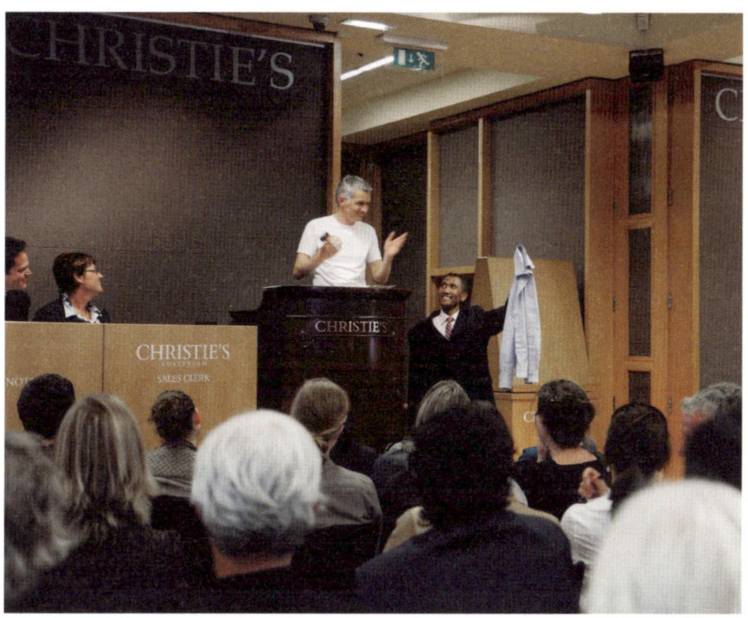

Christian Jankowski, *Strip the Auctioneer*, 2009, C-print, 41 × 50.8 cm, edition of 10, II

In the course of this evolution, the art world has quite clearly become an art industry, at least on its commercial side. As such, it now displays numerous industrial characteristics such as procurement analysis, sales planning, client service, public relations, and brand marketing. Nowhere is this more apparent than in the auction business, where sales are of a public nature and industrial elements become increasingly evident the larger a firm becomes.

But what kind of industry is this actually? There are two large enterprises with business plans: Christie's and Sotheby's. Think Starbucks, or Nespresso. The implementation of the plan is facilitated by direct competitors from the art trade, who have always had a certain entre-

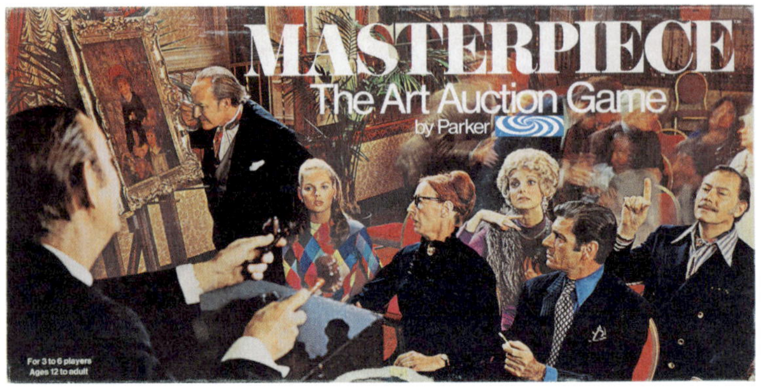

Parker Brothers Inc., Salem, Mass., *Masterpiece: The Art Auction Game*, 1970

preneurial interest in the success of the auction business model, since they can easily use the public validation of art to support their own commercial activities.

When the hammer comes down at auction, it creates a moment of truth, a price achieved in public. This is often explained and almost condoned by the argument that art is merely used as an investment vehicle and that the market is thus manipulated by its participants. However, even the counter-argument – emphasizing the exceptionally high quality of a work of art that sells at a very high price – is only a mitigation masquerading as an explanation. Economically, there is a simple fact: goods were offered and demand has met the supply at a publicly agreed price. This price will remain on record and become a reference point for future sales. The seasonal nature of the auction business enhances the effect, as it creates suspense. As in an Olympic 100-meter sprint, any attempt to break the record can only be made at the next round of games. In the meantime, the historic success becomes both a reference point and an ambition.

The focal point of the process is the figure of the auctioneer. Even if he (or she!) cannot alone create value, the auctioneer's performance has a significant effect on the price of the art work. He strives to turn audience members into bidders engaged in competition, and to this end he makes use of the visceral fascination that auction sales have held over centuries. The ritual dramaturgy of this competition, which is archaic in nature, often creates heart-stopping moments for the participants and grips even neutral observers. It is no surprise that an auction drama features prominently in a recent humorous advertising campaign for a heart medication.[2] In this emotionally charged atmosphere the auctioneer can be compared to a football trainer, who instills his team with the belief that they can win simply because they are better players. The players will believe him if he is a good leader, possibly even disregarding their physical form, and the belief will help them to compete success- fully. The only difference is that there are as many teams in the auction room as there are bidders – and all of them look to the same trainer.

This volume tells the cultural history of the art auction through fourteen individual portraits of auctioneers: one woman and thirteen men. Each describes a particular turning point in the development of auctions. While the selection is representative, it is also driven by the availability of existing sources; many highlights of auctioneering his- tory had to be disregarded. The German reader may miss Heinrich Georg Gutekunst or descriptions of the auctions held at C. G. Börner. The French may look for the attractions of Hôtel Drouot. A New York reader may regret the absence of Hiram Parke of Parke-Bernet or the 1973 sale of the Scull collection at Sotheby's, where works by American contem- porary artists such as Andy Warhol, Willem de Kooning and Robert Rauschenberg were publicly offered for the first time and achieved a record total of $2.2 million.

Little is known about some historic auctioneers, making it harder to record their history. James Christie's innovative approach and charismatic performance have been praised for 250 years, but many of those who followed him lack a profile and sometimes even a name. Only in the second half of the twentieth century did the focus shift to the auctioneer. Brand development as well as the image and reference strategy of the international auction houses since the 1970s have turned the spotlight on individuals who would have remained hidden in the background only a few years earlier. This culminated in the late 1980s, when art and lifestyle converged in a merger of art works and the popular aesthetics of commerce. Art became a subject of the popular press, and the actors in the art market sometimes achieved a status comparable to pop stars. We therefore know relatively little about the group of auctioneers who sold the Hamilton and Beckford collections in 1882 over multiple sessions lasting many days, but the relevant media inform us in great detail about the life, for example, of contemporary auctioneer Tobias Meyer, and not solely about his ability to generate a multi-million dollar turnover in ninety minutes at a New York evening sale.

The acceleration of communication through the Internet, including art market blogs, has increased this trend, and inevitably the term 'star auctioneer' has been coined. Some of these figures are portrayed in this book. But 'auctioneers who made art history' were also the unsung heroes of past centuries. These masters of their trade may have been first and foremost sober tradesmen, but their trade relies in part on raising an emotional temperature. In this setting the audience identifies with them as heroic central characters and projects their passion on to them.

This brief cultural history of the art auction therefore shows a unique development. When auctions were a means of disposing of an

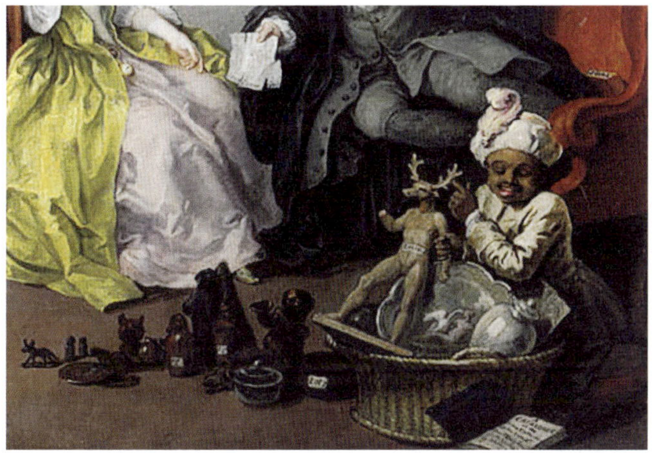

William Hogarth, *The Toilette*, detail of the fourth image in the series
*Marriage à-la-mode*, 1743–45, oil on canvas, 70.5 × 90.8 cm,
National Gallery, London

estate, be it indebted or heirless, or a manner of selling off assets after
a bankruptcy, the business had a dubious reputation. Even in the middle of the eighteenth century, William Hogarth's series of paintings
*Marriage à-la-mode* depicts labelled lots and an auction catalogue in the
household of 'Countess Squanderfield', thus branding auction purchases as the leisure activity of a thoughtless and frivolous class. Even worse,
the source of the purchase is meant to indicate the unsavory and dis-
reputable character of the buyer. Even today the expression 'to come
under the hammer' can imply an undesirable and forced form of asset
disposal. Only in the era of James Christie was an exchange of goods
for money in the saleroom transformed into a social event, which provided a certain entertainment value while also allowing for art appre-
ciation as well as intellectual stimulation. Christie and his followers

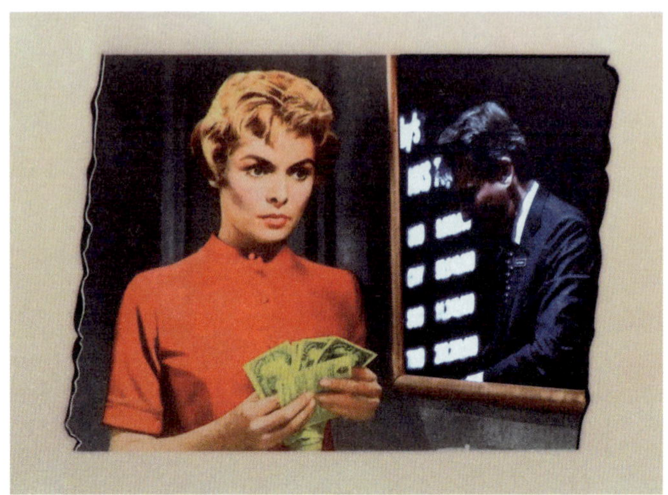

Daniel Cherbuin, *Moronica*, 2013, Photograph, HD-Video

changed the auctioneer from a meticulous and neutral middleman into a charismatic projection figure in society, who inevitably in due course became the subject of artistic reflection himself.

On 20 May 2009 the artist Christian Jankowski arranged a public auction in which Christie's renowned auctioneer Arno Verkade sold the clothes off his own back: *Strip the Auctioneer.* The final lot was the auctioneer's hammer. The exhibition project *The Auction Room*, curated by young designers Mariana Pestana and Designersblock, focused on the design of the objects in this setting. The 2011 event at the London Design Festival presented an entire auction room display including lots, seating, rostrum and hammer, all of which were then sold at the concluding auction.

The auctioneer has also found his way into popular culture, ranging from small porcelain figures (*The Auctioneer* by Royal Doulton) and toys actually modelled on the real auctioneer Simon de Pury (*Action Auctioneer* by the artist The Sucklord) to appearances in such comics as the Walt Disney Company's *Donald Duck: Ducktales* (season 1, episode 25: 'Dr Jekyll & Mr McDuck', 1987) and in the universe of DC Comics (the character of 'Auctioneer' and 'Auctioneer II'). In the area of inter-active games we have the *Gadgetzan Auctioneer* character by Matt Dixon, the iOS game *Auction Wars: Storage King* by GameDigits Ltd, and the countless auctioneers (including one woman) in the multi-player *World of Warcraft*. Real enthusiasts may be able to track down a copy of the 1970s board game *Masterpiece* to enjoy the excitement and glamour of the auction world in the comfort of their own homes.

These examples, no matter how far fetched they are, nonetheless relate to the contributions in this anthology, which round out the se-quence of biographical texts and examine the presence of the auction-eer in everyday life, in fine art, in film and in literature.

# 1   London 1766

Around 1700, the London art market became highly specialised and efficient. Lifting Oliver Cromwell's Puritan laws was an important prerequisite for this development, as all art imports from abroad had previously been prohibited.[3] Once again British aristocrats could, and increasingly did, go on Grand Tours of continental Europe. Above all, the impression these travels made on them formed the basis for their own collecting activities. An art collection soon became an indispensable asset to maintain a prestigious position in society. The country's beginning supremacy in European trade channelled large funds into its economy. While the Italian aristocracy became impoverished and had to sell, the British aristocracy became established buyers.[4]

From the middle of the century, London and Paris dominated other cultural centres last not least because of the supply required by the royal courts as well as increasing demand from the wealthy middle class.[5] At the beginning of the eighteenth century educational tours took the art lover to the sites of classical antiquity, while the art buyer travelled to London and Paris. The art trade responded by opening up to this development. Showrooms invited the visitor to linger and enjoy the pleasure of looking at art; they became places of intellectualisation through stimulating exchange across social classes.[6]

The 1760s therefore marked a turning point in England. As the Royal Academy was founded, the first Annual Exhibitions encouraged the enjoyment as well as the consumption of art. The competition between the London and Paris markets influenced art prices, with consequent implications for the European auction business.[7] The oldest auction house of that era still in existence today is Auktionsverket, founded in Stockholm in 1674. The Vienna Dorotheum opened in 1707, initially as a pawnbroker. Even the London firm of Sotheby's had a very different profile at the time. Until the twentieth century the house specialised exclusively in book sales.[8] London auction sales took place only during the town season from September to May. The upper classes were in the country over the summer, and business ceased. The traditional German saying, *Kirschen rot, Handel tot* ('cherries are red, when business is dead') did not just apply to the art trade. Indeed, this schedule continues to set the rhythms of the auction market today.

The London art market was buoyed considerably by the French Revolution and the Napoleonic wars, since this was where emigrating aristocrats could sell their only moveable possessions: art works and jewellery. Between 1790 and 1820 several important continental collections were sold in London, such as Calonne, Conti, Lafitte, and Orléans. Highlights were the sales of Countess du Barry's jewels at Christie's and the Talleyrand collection at Philips.[9] At the same time, a number of dealerships sprung up, such as those of Old Masters dealers Paul Colnaghi, Arthur J. Sulley and, in 1817, Agnew's, where art works saved from the French Revolution found British buyers.[10]

Representing the economic system of this market through financial analysis is rather daunting. A world record price of a kind for the period seems to have been paid by Augustus the Strong for Raphael's Sistine Madonna, at least according to the views of contemporary commentators, who described £8,500 as extraordinary.[11]

## 1  James Christie
## The Power of Place, Promotion and Personality

In a business prone to secrecy and not averse to hyperbole, separating myth from reality to explain the success of an auction house presents a challenge. In the case of Christie's, the difficulties are compounded by the destruction of its historical archives – apart from a set of annotated sale catalogues – when a bomb fell on the King Street saleroom in April 1941. Furthermore, the origins of its founder, James Christie, are so shrouded in mystery as to suggest a conscious effort on his part to obscure them. But it is clear that he was the right man in the right place at the right time, and before his death on 8 November 1803, he had raised the business of art auctioneering to new prominence.[12]

From his short obituary in the *Gentleman's magazine*, it seems he was born in 1730. The earliest Christie auction to be traced dates from 1760, and 'Christie' based in Oxford Road [Street] is listed among the twenty-two auctioneers in Mortimer's *Universal Director* of 1763.[13] Of those who dealt in art, the most successful were Abraham Langford, established in the Great Piazza, Covent Garden, and John Prestage, who held picture sales in a 'Great Room' in Savile Row. The deaths of Prestage in 1767, Langford in 1776 and the leading art dealer, Dr Robert Bragge, the following year, helped to clear the field for Christie.[14]

Although he was still based off Oxford Street, his sale of the property of a 'Noble Personage (Deceas'd)' on 5–9 December 1766 took place

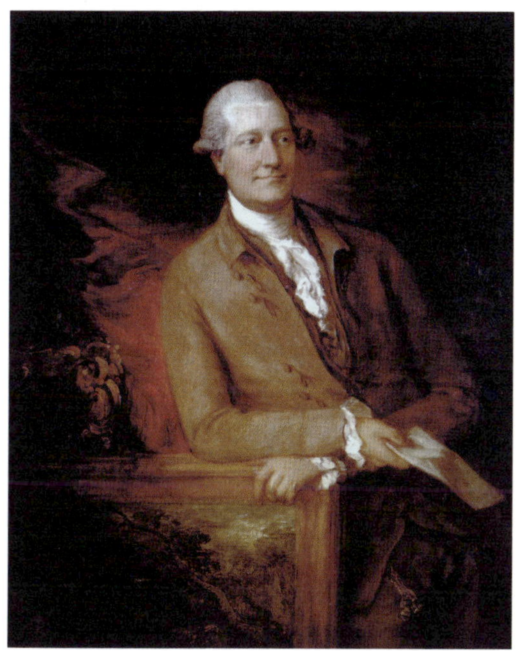

Thomas Gainsborough, *James Christie*, 1778, oil on canvas,
126 × 102 cm, The J. Paul Getty Museum, Los Angeles

at 'the Auction Room, in Pall Mall'. The move of his home and business
to Pall Mall the following year was a clear signal that he intended to rise
in the world. Connecting Haymarket to St James's Street, it could not
have been a more propitious location in the social geography of the metropolis. There were three royal residences on the south side – St James's
Palace at the west end, Carlton House at the east and newly built Cumberland House in the middle. On the north side, in William Almack's
rooms at nos. 49–50, the most fashionable London clubs were having
their early meetings. Testing the market before acquiring his own prem-

ises, Christie held his first Pall Mall sales in the 'Great Room' at the eastern Haymarket end, no. 125, leased in 1765 to George III's librarian, Richard Dalton, to serve as a print warehouse.[15] In 1768, he himself leased nos. 83–84 Pall Mall, nearer Almack's but still on the south side, sandwiched between Schomberg House to the west and Cumberland House to the east.[16] He spent a thousand pounds on alterations, erecting a 'spacious and lofty' auction room in the garden to the rear, completed by the end of 1768.[17] The cachet of Pall Mall increased further when, in 1783, Carlton House was presented to the Prince of Wales on attaining his majority, and after extensive improvements it became the hub of high society.[18]

In Pall Mall, Christie also had his finger on the pulse of the contemporary art world. The newly founded Royal Academy held its first meeting in Dalton's rooms at no. 125 in December 1768 and its first exhibition there the following summer. But Dalton could not make a financial go of it and assigned his lease to Christie in 1771 with a restrictive covenant safeguarding the Academy's continued use of the space for its annual exhibitions, which were held there until 1779. For more than thirty years Christie used one or other of his Pall Mall 'Great Rooms' for auctions, splitting the sale of Sir Joshua Reynolds's pictures in March 1795 between them and sometimes renting out no. 125.[19] Until 1774, the rival Free Society of Artists used Christie's premises at nos. 83–84 for its annual exhibitions. Leading artists lived in the neighbourhood, notably Gainsborough in the west wing of Schomberg House from 1774 until his death in 1788. With artists not only producing works but also collecting and dealing in them, to be at the centre of the art scene was crucial. It has been calculated that Christie staged thirty-two sales of artists' property between 1766 and 1803.[20] Artists were also more trusted than most to pronounce on the merit of pictures for sale.

Christie joined an ever-growing circuit of attractions that kept fashionable West End society amused during the Season. In the wake of the successes of the Seven Years' War, London was 'swinging' with unprecedented confidence. Besides the round of theatres, clubs, pleasure gardens and, from 1772, the splendid new Pantheon in Oxford Street, shopping for luxury goods had never been more appealing. Commercially-minded entrepreneurs competed to relieve the nobility, gentry and aspiring middle-classes of their funds, either in their own showrooms or in those of the auctioneers or both. At a time when luxury retailing was still a novelty, stock control in its infancy, cash flow uncertain and bankruptcy ever threatening, Christie performed an extremely valuable service. His 'Great Rooms' operated as a superior sort of outlet village, disposing of goods whose fashionable moment had peaked but were not yet ready for recall to their places of manufacture. From 1767 onwards he sold: the surplus stock of assorted china-men, including Nicholas Sprimont's Chelsea porcelain and the Chelsea and Derby ware of his successor, William Duesbury; Boulton and Fothergill's ormolu-mounted vases, candlesticks and perfume burners 'of exquisite workmanship and finished in the antique taste' in 1770, 1771 and 1778; items from James Cox's Museum of bejewelled mechanical marvels following his bankruptcy in 1779; and Josiah Wedgwood's basalt busts and jasperware in 1781, following the death of his partner, Thomas Bentley. In addition to such leading 'brands', he auctioned off the stock-in-trade of businesses that were closing down – artificial stone ornaments, jewellery, plate and fashion accessories, glassware, hats and millinery, broadcloth, lace and Spitalfields silks.

Christie could not afford to be fussy about his clientele and was prepared to travel to the suburbs and provinces to take sales on site, including the live and dead stock on a Hampshire farm. London house sales were based mainly in the West End – Mayfair and St James's, Marylebone and Soho. Where he could, he named titled owners. Probably the largest was the twelve-day sale that took place in December 1775 of the contents of Holland House in Kensington, following the death of Henry Fox, 1st Baron Holland, which so distressed Horace Walpole he could not bear to attend.[21] In situ sales of household furniture, plate, china, linen, wines etcetera constitute by far the largest category of catalogue in the archives, and they provided Christie's bread-and-butter throughout his career.

While Christie was only one of many auctioneers capable of disposing of household goods and surplus stock, by the end of the 1770s he seemed to be well on the way to dominating the market in pictures. Following the Peace of Paris, the import of paintings (mainly from Italy) rose to over a thousand a year.[22] Among those bringing them in were Robert Ansell (c.1732–1789) and Robert Strange (1725–1792), who in turn supplied Christie. Besides providing the aristocracy with picture frames and furniture, Ansell staged a picture sale at Christie's each February from 1768 to 1772, the contents described as 'consigned from abroad'. The earliest of these sales was the first Christie picture sale to attract a sprinkling of nobility among the buyers. Ansell might have been related to the James Ansell, who witnessed Christie's marriage in 1772 and was his business partner from January 1777 until October 1784.

In 1769 Robert Strange, the leading line-engraver of his day, issued a descriptive catalogue of the pictures he had acquired during his travels in France and Italy, prior to their dispersal in two sales held at Christie's in 1771 and 1773. The latter included Poussin's *Landscape with a man killed by a snake*, which went to Sir Watkin Williams-Wynn for £650,[23] and the last lot in the sale, Claude Lorrain's *Landscape with the voyage of*

*Jacob*, bought for the Earl of Chesterfield, then virtually on his deathbed, by his valet for 400 guineas.[24] In a letter of 1 May 1774, Horace Walpole expressed his astonishment at the prices now paid at auction: 'Next to gaming, which subsides a little from want of materials, the predominant folly is pictures – I beg their pardon for associating them with gaming. Sir George Colbrooke, a citizen, and martyr to what is called *speculation*, had his pictures sold by auction last week.'[25]

The success of the Ansell and Strange sales attracted a string of prestigious remnants from the estates of deceased foreign grandees, while ambassadors to the court of St James found Christie's a convenient place to dispose of their plate, china and wine cellars before returning home. Between 1776 and 1794 the firm sold the property of ambassadors from Hanover, Spain, Naples, France, Holland (two), Denmark, Prussia and Sweden.

Dealers such as Anstell, John Bertels (1727–1792) and Benjamin Vandergucht (1752–1794) supplied Christie's, among others, with pictures they procured on the Paris or Antwerp markets.[26] A great deal of recycling went on in the trade, and Christie also handled dealers' posthumous stock sales.[27] The letters of William Buchanan (1777–1864) provide insight into how they used the firm, bringing a 'parcel' of Italian imports 'forward at Christie's at a period of the year when people are full of money.' Pictures were consigned which were not so likely 'to go off rapidly by private sale'; so in effect, dealers used Christie's like the manufacturers of luxury goods, to dispose of end-of-line stock.[28] Nevertheless, dealers' rings could also keep prices low. When works imported from Rome by the artist James Irvine fell victim to such tactics at Christie's on 24 March 1792, he complained to a friend, 'All agree that so compleat an instance of villainy and underhand dealing never came within their knowledge.'[29]

Christie was not the first auctioneer to stage fashionable sales. Bragge's sales had attracted the nobility and gentry in the late 1740s and 1750s, as did Langford's sale in 1758 of the pictures owned by the deceased diplomat Sir Luke Schaub.[30] But he was peculiarly aware of the power of promotion, to the point of becoming, in June 1769, one of the twenty original proprietors of the Whig *Morning Chronicle* and taking a share in the Tory *Morning Post* three years later. In his advance notices and on the title pages of his catalogues, an illustrious provenance was emphasised, even if anonymous. The world could easily identify the 'Person of great Rank', whose 'superb jewels, trinkets, plate, gold and silver medals, china &c' were sold on 1–3 February 1773, as Augusta of Saxe-Gotha, late Princess of Wales (1719–1772).

Some sales of effects had celebrity or notoriety appeal, as in the case of the actor Samuel Foote in 1778, Dr Johnson's library in 1785, the bigamous Duchess of Kingston, whose jewels went in 1791 for £7,400, or the books and manuscripts of the transvestite Chevalier D'Eon the same year. (The title-page of Christie's catalogue for the latter sale referred to him as the Chevalière D'Eon and to 'her' library, 'household furniture, swords, trinkets, jewels, and, in general, all her wearing apparel, constituting the Wardrobe of a Captain of Dragoons and a French Lady.'[31]) A 'most capital and superb assemblage of valuable jewels, of the most singular excellence, beauty and perfection' was sold on 19 February 1795 'late the property of Madame La Comtesse DuBarry, deceased'. Having been stolen in Paris and smuggled to London, the jewels could not be retrieved before she was guillotined. They went for £8,791. James Gillray could not resist caricaturing the glamorous previews such sales attracted. *A Peep at Christies*, published in 1796, depicted a diminutive Earl of Derby with his constant companion, the actress Elizabeth Farren, 'Taking the morning Lounge'.[32]

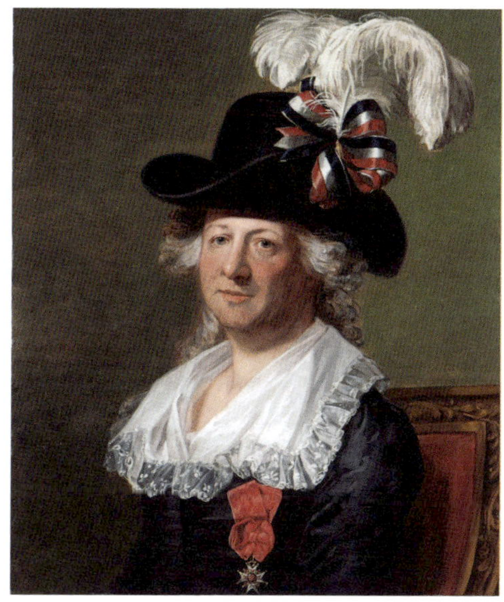

Thomas Stewart, after Jean Laurent Mosnier, *Chevalier d'Eon*, 1792, oil on canvas, 76.5 × 64 cm, National Portrait Gallery, London

The title pages of Christie's quarto- or foolscap-size picture catalogues were interlaced with superlatives of all kinds – 'most capital and valuable collection … by the most esteemed Masters … in the highest state of perfection,' etcetera. They were usually followed by a simple list of artists and works, but the Strange sales elaborated on the format with an introduction and their owner's description of individual works. The 1795 sale catalogue of Sir Joshua Reynolds's collection was prefaced with a statement from his executors, led by Edmund Burke, who again talked up the artist's taste and judgement.

Major sales were organised to culminate in a climax, the most valuable pictures being kept back until the final lots, attracting private buyers fashionably late in the day.

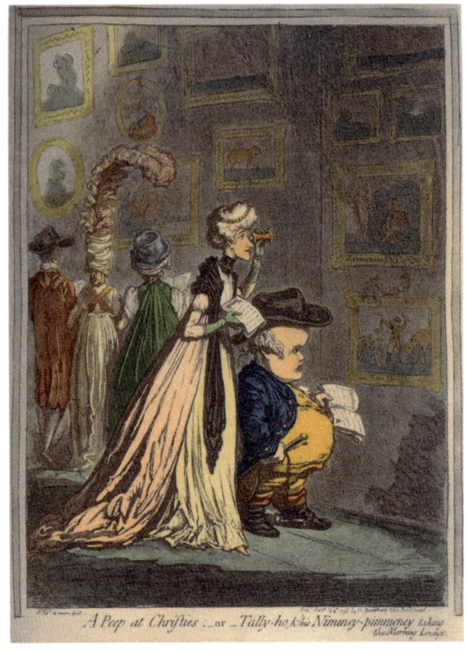

James Gillray, *A Peep at Christies: or Tally-ho & his Nimeney-pimmeney, Taking the morning Lounge*, 24 September 1796

In Richard Brinsley Sheridan's satire *The Critic* (1779), the claims made by Puff, the playwright, that he was the first to enrich the literary style of auctioneers suggest it was a novel phenomenon: ' 'twas I first taught them to crowd their advertisements with panegyrical superlatives, each epithet rising above the other, like the bidders in their own auction-rooms! From me they learned to inlay their phraseology with variegated chips of exotic metaphor: by me too their inventive faculties were called forth.' Furthermore, Christie was eloquent on the rostrum, a master of saleroom patter. First caricatured in a satirical print entitled *Eloquence or The King of Epithets*, published in 1782, he was dubbed 'The

Specious Orator' in Robert Dighton's squib of 1794.[33] Much has been made recently of the 'rhetorical strategies' he employed in his theatrical performances on the rostrum. Stimulating the audience to re-imagine or reconstruct the world from which the goods came, it has been argued, he legitimised their redistribution through suggesting an imagined change in social identity.[34]

The journalist and critic John Taylor recalled, 'There was something interesting and persuasive, as well as thoroughly agreeable in his manner. He was very animated and it may be justly said, eloquent, in his recommendation of any article to be announced from his "Rostrum", as well as in occasional effusions of genuine humour.'[35] Tall and dignified in appearance, he was perceived as 'gentlemanlike', if not 'gentlemanly'. Gainsborough's portrait of his Pall Mall neighbour is slyly revealing. Dating from 1778, it shows Christie leaning on one of the artist's landscapes and grasping onto its frame, while glancing somewhat furtively to one side as if wondering how he could dispose of it.[36]

Joseph Farington reported that Christie had a very good head for scheming but lacked education.[37] Even his most eulogistic admirers are hard-pressed to describe him as a connoisseur, but he knew how to make use of the knowledge of others, especially artists. Besides, although the licensing of auctioneers was introduced in 1777, the authenticity of a work was not subject to legal definition unless deliberate fraud could be established. In the then state of expertise, caveat emptor prevailed, and buyers were more reassured by an illustrious provenance than by connoisseurship. The lawsuit brought in 1787 by Noël Desenfans against his fellow dealer Benjamin Vandergucht for selling him a dud Poussin reveals that even artists and connoisseurs could be equivocal and unreliable witnesses in a court of law, although Desanfans won the case.[38]

When asked by the 3rd Earl of Orford to value the collection formed by Sir Robert Walpole, prior to its sale to the Empress Catherine II of Russia, Christie employed the bankrupt artist and printmaker Philip Joseph Tassaert (1732–1803) as well as Royal Academicians, Giovanni Battista Cipriani and Benjamin West. Bitterly disappointed by the imminent sale, Horace Walpole considered his father's collection overvalued and was unimpressed by the judgement of those who had made the estimates, doubting the authenticity of some works: 'In short the appraisers were determined to consider what the Czarina *could* give, rather than what the pictures were really worth.' Nevertheless, the sale was agreed on the basis of Christie's final valuation of £40,555, although it is not clear how much the Empress paid in the end.[39]

His success is less obvious in terms of the major collections of pictures that poured into London, with or without their hapless owners, following the outbreak of the French Revolution. The sale of the pictures of Charles-Alexandre de Calonne, mortgaged to the dealers Noël Desenfans and Michael Byran to finance the emigré cause, was handled in March 1795 by Skinner and Dyke.[40] Philippe, duc d'Orléans, badly in debt yet desperate to finance his political ambitions, sought to sell his famed collection of Old Masters in England as early as 1790. With Bertels and Vandergucht also sniffing round, Christie secretly dispatched Tassaert to Paris. He reported back that if Christie could buy the collection for £30,000–40,000, he might make a fortune.[41] But nothing came of it, and in 1792 a collector and speculator, Thomas Moore Slade, managed to acquire the Dutch, Flemish and German works for a consortium led by Lord Kinnaird. When 259 pictures were put on sale at 125 Pall Mall in 1793, crowds flocked to see them. The Italian and French pictures were acquired for £43,000 through the London dealer, Michael Bryan, by a syndicate comprising the 3rd Duke of Bridgewater, his nephew Earl

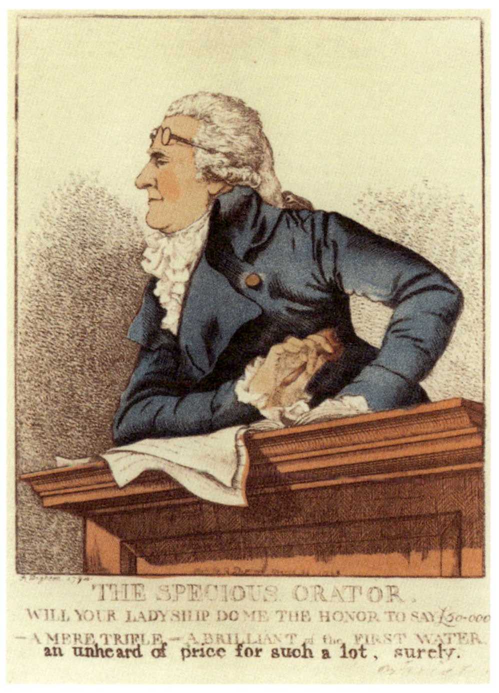



Robert Dighton,
*The Specious Orator*, 1794

Gower and Gower's brother-in-law, the 5th Earl of Carlisle. Christie must have been grinding his teeth when the smaller pictures were displayed virtually next door, from December 1798 to July 1799, at no. 88 Pall Mall, not to mention the larger ones at the Lyceum in the Strand.[42]

Comments made by Joseph Farington around this time – and Christie's failure to snare the Calonne and Orléans collections – may indicate that he was hard-pressed for cash.[43] A partnership with William Sharp, a leading City diamond merchant and Thomas Harper, a Fleet Street goldsmith and prominent freemason, was short-lived, from 16 February to 20 May 1797. Nevertheless, Christie disposed of several collections of fine French porcelain and, in February 1797, sold the French and Dutch pictures acquired from French aristocrats by the Connecticut-born artist, John Trumbull, while attached to the American legation in Paris.[44] Referring to the convulsions with which France had been distracted, the confusion of persons and property, the catalogue introduction observed, 'England has had, perhaps, the greatest share in gathering up these scattered Treasures, and by affording a Sanctuary to the Fine Arts, has constituted within herself an Emporium of Wealth, incalculable.'

The firm was to scoop up more art treasures as war spread to Italy.[45] In 1794, Christie's oldest son, the Eton-educated antiquary James Christie junior (1773–1831), took his first auction and was increasingly active in the business. Christie senior had founded and built it up through hard work and energetic entrepreneurship, seizing the opportunities presented in a new consumer-orientated society and associating at least the Christie name with the luminaries of the age – aristocrats, celebrities, artists, collectors and manufacturers. His flair for marketing and his engaging personality on the rostrum were key elements in his success, supported by sufficient reputation for probity to achieve respectability and to be recommended with some confidence. It was now for his genteel scholarly son to consolidate Christie's position as the world's leading fine art saleroom.

## 2 Pompeii 1875

While the beginnings of the art market are buried in the dark recesses of history, it is rooted in Egyptian and Phoenician trade relations with a wide variety of neighbouring peoples, and verifiable since circa 1,500 B.C. At the time, art works were not private property but decorated temples and altars. We have no evidence of any secular private collecting activity.[46] In classical Greece, however, we know that copies of images of deities were sold to the faithful at places of worship.[47] Artists themselves had relatively minor social standing, although they were regarded as instruments of the Gods, who communicated through their creative work.[48]

The first important collectors emerged in the Hellenistic period and in ancient Rome. Both the kings of Pergamon and the Egyptian pharaohs assembled collections of art works they had been given, purchased, or looted. Actual private collectors were to appear only in the ruling class of Rome. Art works were war booty and therefore exhibited and later also sold for prestige purposes. The great esteem among Romans for Greek art in particular, however, soon led to a collecting culture that was no longer tied to the representation of military victory. By the time of the Roman Empire at the latest, the requirements of any educated and wealthy Roman included the possession of an art collection. [49]

In order to meet demand, it did not take long for a limited art market to be established. The Roman street best known for its high density of art dealers was the Via Saepta Iulia. The Roman art dealer Iunius Damasippus achieved prominence, not so much for the Greek antiquities he offered but for his spectacular bankruptcy as recounted by Horace in his Satires.[50] There are also contemporary reports of forgeries of such Greek antiquities.[51] Art dealing was often a side line for other commercial activities; any specialised sellers of art were likely to be the artists themselves offering their own work.[52]

The market in general, however, seems to have been highly specialised. Collecting art was an exclusive pursuit even by today's standards. Prices for works of applied art as quoted by Cicero are even comparable to those paid for the works by French cabinet-makers in the last third of the nineteenth century.[53] Other contemporary writers also highlight auctions and auction prices. Around 500 B.C. there are reports of brides being auctioned in Babylon.[54] The Greek island of Delos appears to have been the centre of the antique auction market for slaves. Nevertheless, apart from slaves, the wares offered in Rome were mostly victuals, and rather less frequently, art works and furnishings.[55] The term itself derives from the Latin *auctio*, meaning augmentation, and indicates an auction model with increasing bids.

Only with a spectacular find made during the Pompeii excavations of 1875 did details of such transactions become known to the modern world ...

## 2   Lucius Caecilius Iucundus
##     Messages from the Art Market in Antiquity

When doors open in the course of history to reveal a glimpse of distant spheres in time or space, there has always been a major impact on the intellectual history of mankind. The travel reports of Marco Polo and Christopher Columbus, the discovery of Tutankhamun's tomb, and the first moon landing are all examples of events of considerable impact. This is especially true of the discovery in 1748 of Pompeii and Herculaneum, which provided remarkable insight into everyday life in Roman antiquity in 79 A.D., the year lava from Vesuvius swept over those cities and preserved them for posterity.

The royal family of the Kingdom of Naples initially exercised the strictest control over access to the site. Even so, the news spread through Europe like wildfire, not least through prints. These were expensive but relatively easy to distribute, and both scholars and dilettanti soon travelled to Italy to study the buried world and publish their own experiences and findings.[56] Antiques became as collectible as *Kunstkammer* objects had been in the previous century. In general, this greatly influenced modern concepts of collecting, conserving and researching art and shaped the quintessence of today's museums. The first antiquities the British Museum purchased after its foundation were the so-called 'Etruscan' vases excavated in Southern Italy that Sir William Hamilton had collected while serving as the British ambassador in Naples.

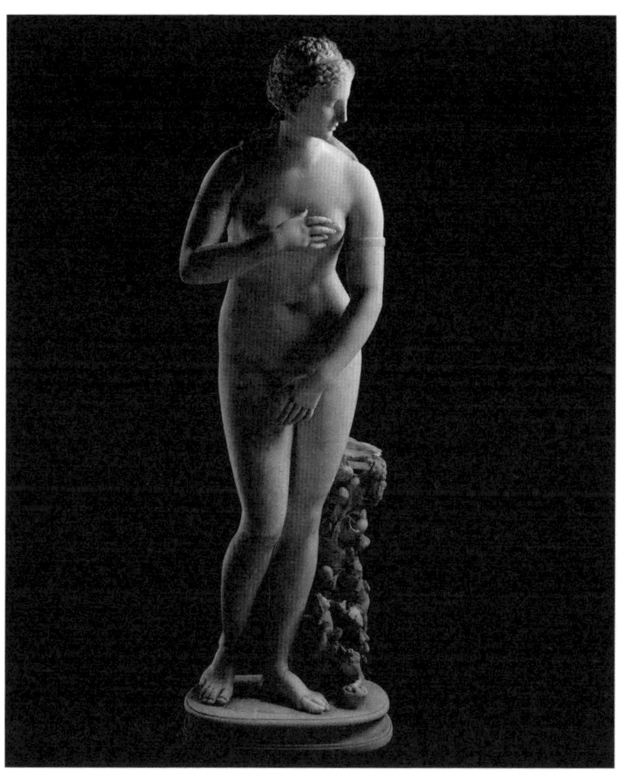

*Venus Medici*, also called the *Jenkins-Venus*, marble, first half of 2nd century AD (Roman copy after the Greek original), height: 162 cm

The sensational finds at Pompeii and Herculaneum immediately led to a wave of enthusiasm for antiquity as well as to increased travel to the region.[57] The excavation process, however, took more than a century to complete. This was mostly due to the limited technical means available as well as to the area's enormous expanse.[58] Moreover, after almost two millennia in darkness, many of the ancient walls gave way and collapsed

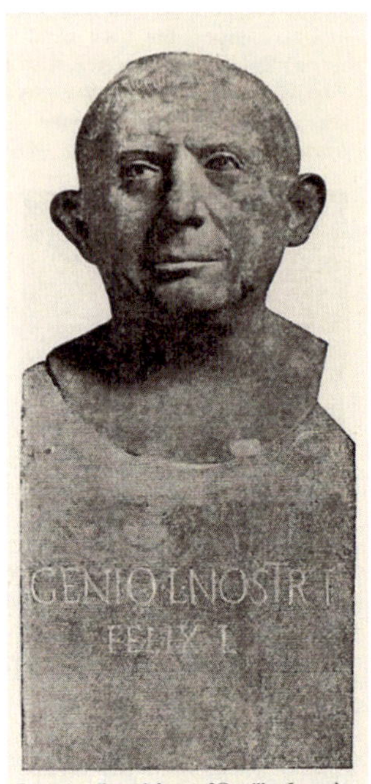

Fig. 246. — Portrait herm of Caecilius Jucundus.

Portrait herm of Lucius Caecilius Iucundus from the atrium of his house on Via Stabia, Pompeii, bronze and marble; illustration from August Mau, *Pompeii: Its Life and Art*, 1899

when they were finally exposed again to the elements, which in turn opened up additional levels for excavation and uncovered further artefacts. It is therefore not surprising that a major discovery in the city of Pompeii was not made until 1875: the documents of Lucius Caecilius Iucundus. The Roman banker and auctioneer not only kept meticulous business records but also made provisions for the safekeeping of his files. This find opened an important window onto the workings of auctions and financial transactions in antiquity.

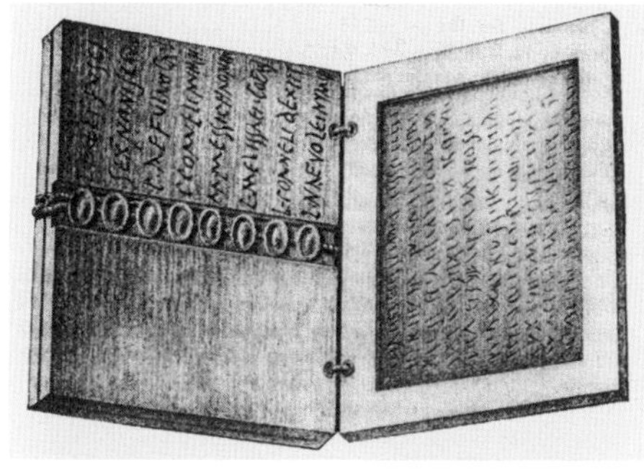

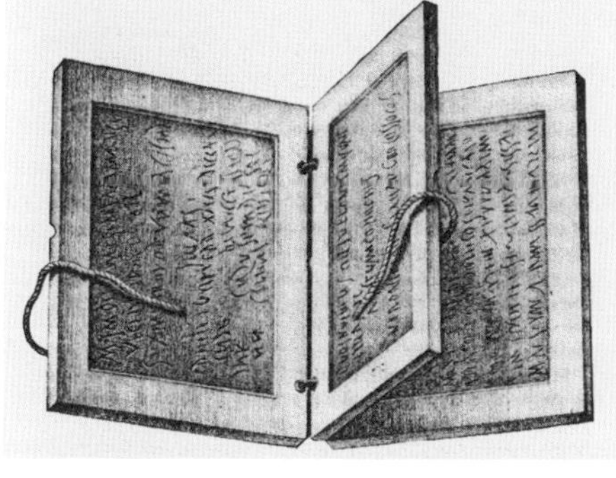

Wax tablets belonging to
Lucius Caecilius Iucundus;
illustrations from August Mau,
*Pompeii: Its Life and Art,* 1899

In all, 153 small wax tablets bound together in diptychs or triptychs
were stored in a wooden crate with extensive metal casing, which mostly withstood the heat of the volcanic ash fall.[59] Iucundus's records were
typical of the Roman Empire in that they consisted of boxwood panels
coated on one side with wax. This surface was engraved with a stylus;
if space ran out on the panel, however, the writing often continued on
the edge or the back of the tablet. This was done in ink. The wax of course
melted in the heat of the volcanic eruption, but the ink inscriptions

survived, mainly providing information about individual business transactions.[60]

As with the art trade in general, auctions in antiquity were mostly a sideline, secondary to other business activities. Lucius Caecilius Iucundus was mainly a banker, sometimes also a tax collector.[61] The tablets consist of receipts from people for whom he conducted auctions. They offer deep insight into the structure of such a business. One is struck by the parallels with modern auctioneering. Through ancient writers such as Pliny, Cicero and Cato the Elder we know that objects were auctioned when an estate was dissolved or when an owner could not pay his debts.[62] From the times of Emperor Augustus onwards, such auctions were taxed at a rate of 1 per cent. Even at that time, the seller in the transaction was represented by a professional intermediary, known as the *coactor*. The buyer in turn paid the mediator with a *merces*, a fee of another per cent. Later Roman sources found in Portugal confirm that, at a later stage, there was definitely a sliding scale: the charges for transactions below a certain threshold were 2 per cent; above it the buyer's premium was only 1 per cent. Basic flat fees were applied for objects whose sale required a disproportionate effort in relation to their sale price.[63] The *coactor* would then deduct all costs as well as the auction tax from the purchase price and pay out the remaining proceeds to the vendor.

In addition to the *coactor*, a banker known as the *argentarius* maintained overall financial control and oversight for the auction; these two roles could also be filled by the same person. This supervisory function can be most closely compared to that of today's *Ammann* or *huissier* who still oversee auctions in Switzerland and France. However, an *argentarius* could also advance the vendor the sale price, a concept comparable to a backer or a contemporary 'third party guarantor'.[64] The banker

Lucius Caecilius Iucundus is described as such a *coactor argentarius*.[65] The actual sale was however conducted by the *praeco*, who also knocked down the winning bid.[66] It seems that the double role of the auctioneer was still divided in two: on the one hand, the neutral intermediary between buyer and seller, and on the other hand, the master of ceremonies for the selling process.[67]

The details obtained from Iucundus's documents demonstrate that auctions were a central part of the Roman economy and were used on a daily basis to bring about an expeditious handling of goods. Although some steps in the auctioneering process are still divided among several players, the first century A.D. was already familiar with the basics of a distribution system that still plays a central role in today's art market. Even if the appearance of auctions has undergone considerable changes, the essential structure of the selling process has basically remained the same. In other words, the old adage of the 'archaic rivalry' in the saleroom is not just a metaphor.

## 3   London 1882

The modern art market in Europe developed over the course of the nineteenth century. The first public museums and art societies were an essential prerequisite to this development.[68] The museum in the Louvre, which had been founded in 1793, became the first institution to define the four objectives – collecting, preserving, researching and communicating – and according to Voltaire fulfilled the role of a temple of good taste.[69] The principles remain valid to this day. However, as the Louvre collected older art, the first institute for contemporary art was founded in the Palais du Luxembourg in 1818. Simultaneously, early historic and antiquarian societies sprang up in Germany. For the first time citizens were involved in the public collection and exhibition of art, not least encouraging a private interest in art and passion for collecting in bourgeois circles.[70] Demand on the art market grew with the rise in economic power of the bourgeoisie. The first Great Exhibition at the Crystal Palace in London in 1851 sought to meet aesthetic requirements around the decoration of upper middle-class homes with works of the beaux arts and the *arts utiles*, respectively. In its Wunderkammer-style displays was born the format of a commercial fair, which lives on in the art and antiquity fairs of the twenty-first century.[71]

Today's art market is mainly rooted in three almost simultaneous developments: the economic rise of the United States after its war of independence, the revision of the British inheritance tax laws in the second half of the nineteenth century, and the influence of the Impressionists in France.[72] The history of the Hamilton Palace auction and subsequent auction sales illustrates the influence of the Settled Land Act on changes in the legal framework for estate sales as well as the changing behaviour patterns of an international clientele of buyers.[73] British landowners had become impoverished as a consequence of the European market being flooded with cheap American wheat. When bankruptcies increased, the inheritance legislation was changed to allow an estate to be rescued through the sale of its art treasures.

These riches now began to pour into the London auction rooms, underpinning their dominant position in Europe. At the same time, the United States had developed economically to such an extent that wealthy Americans could enter the European scene as collectors and buyers for these objects.

The following three decades are often described as the golden age of the art trade and are characterised by the high esteem in which the work of French cabinetmakers was held.[74] Prices that strike us as extraordinary, including those paid for decorative art objects in the Hamilton Palace auction, were based on the cost of replacement, i.e. contemporary production costs.[75] These were not just theoretical assumptions as copies of historic pieces were also made and sold. The passion for objects for interiors in the classical French style would only abate after the First World War – and then in favour of fine art.

## 3    The Hamilton Palace Sale and a Global Market

On Saturday 17 June 1882, London buzzed with excitement. A steady stream of carriages flowed towards Christie's on King Street, keenly observed by newspaper reporters eager to note the identity of their occupants. Meanwhile the saleroom thronged with a growing crowd of aristocrats, bankers, industrialists, art dealers and museum officials all jostling for space before the rostrum.

The occasion was the Hamilton Palace sale, and bidding was about to start on the first of over two thousand lots which, in the course of seventeen days, would raise almost £400,000; a sum that would not be matched in the salerooms for thirty years.

Hamilton Palace, the principal seat of the Dukes of Hamilton, Scotland's premier peers, was located about ten miles southeast of Glasgow. It had been enlarged in the 1820s to suit the princely tastes of Alexander, 10th Duke of Hamilton (1767–1852), who filled its new state rooms with Old Master paintings, French royal furniture, Napoleonic silver and other luxurious objects which aligned the palace's inhabitants with the ruling dynasties of European history. The collection was further augmented in 1844 with a large bequest from the 10th duke's father-in-law, William Beckford (1760–1844). By 1882 the palace stood as a monument to the status of the dukes and the wealth they had derived from the coalfields on their estates in the Central Belt of Scotland.

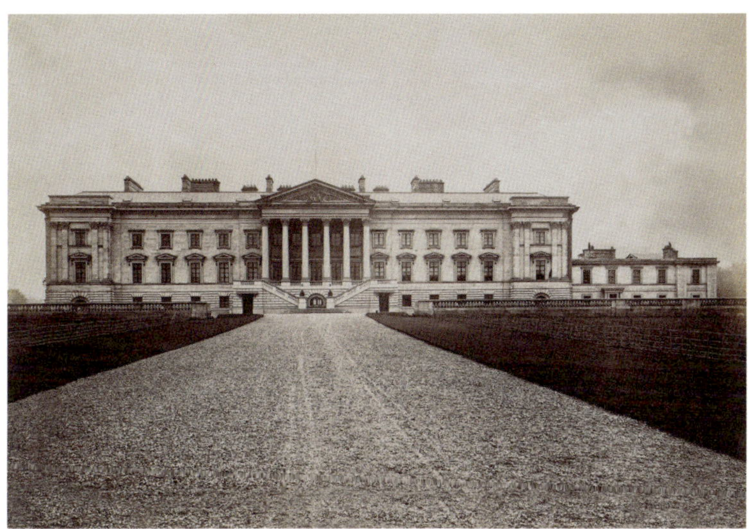

The approach to the north front of Hamilton Palace (demolished after 1920), photograph by Thomas Annan, before 1882, National Museums of Scotland, Edinburgh

The Hamilton Palace sale is considered a landmark in auction history because it coincided with the passing of the Settled Land Act. By the closing decades of the nineteenth century, an increasingly global economy and cheap agricultural imports from America had begun to seriously undermine the economic supremacy of the British landed classes. The traditional trinity of land, wealth and power was broken, and in 1882 the British government threw a lifeline to its struggling aristocracy. This new piece of legislation enabled the land-owning classes to avoid financial ruin by voluntarily selling entailed property, both territorial and material, which they had previously been obliged by law to preserve for their successors. Although the Hamilton Palace sale occurred several months before the Settled Land Act came into effect,

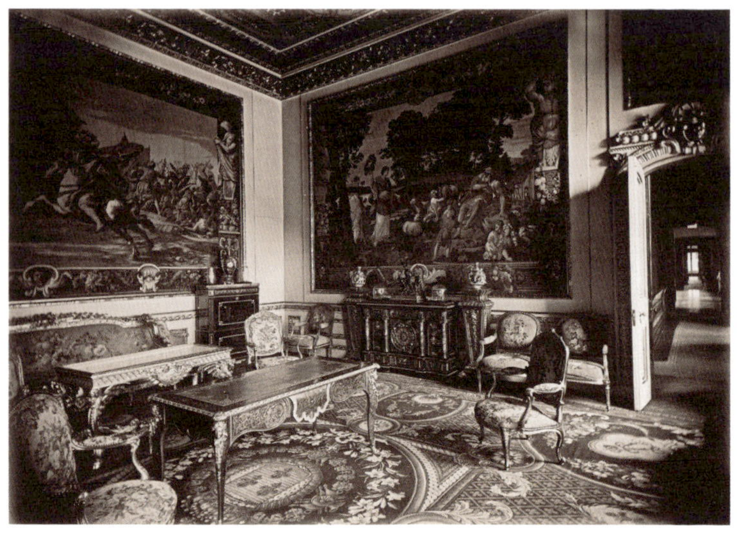

The New State Drawing Room, photograph by Thomas Annan, before 1882, National Museums of Scotland, Edinburgh.

and so was not a direct consequence of this new legislation, it seems the 12th Duke of Hamilton, with the help of an astute commissioner, had identified a loophole in the conditions of his entail which enabled him to consign his ancestral art collection to auction. Furthermore, his financial necessity had little to do with the agricultural depression, for the ducal revenue came largely from coal mining. His debts of over one million pounds were principally the result of a fondness for racehorses and expensive yachts. Therefore, the circumstances of the Hamilton Palace sale were little different from those of the forced dispersals of previous generations, such as Wanstead House (1822), Fonthill Abbey (1822) and Stowe House (1848). It was excess, rather than privation, that brought the treasures of Hamilton Palace to the saleroom.

Although it narrowly preceded the passing of the Settled Land Act, the dispersal of the Hamilton Palace collection heralded a new era of 'voluntary' country house sales, which thereafter became an ever-increasing fixture of the salerooms. It brought a supernova of artistic treasures to the art market, the scope of which had not been seen in over a generation. Its principal glory was the eighteenth-century French furniture, but the sale also included important Dutch, Flemish, Italian, Spanish and French Old Master paintings, fine silver-gilt, clocks, Japanese lacquer, Chinese porcelain, rock crystal and other objects of vertu. Many of the most significant items are now the highlights of museums, galleries and libraries around the world.

A further distinguishing characteristic of this sale is the unprecedented snapshot it presents of the art market at a time of great social and economic change. The mix of aristocrats, plutocrats, international art dealers and museum officials reported in the saleroom was, in 1882, a new phenomenon. As the country responded to the growing effects of globalisation, the London salerooms inevitably became a meeting point for a society in flux, as the old order yielded its ancestral riches to a glittering array of increasingly international plutocrats. Although the landed classes were not an entirely spent force, their economic means (where not reinvigorated by marital alliances with banking or industry) were ever diminished. In short, no longer did the British aristocracy and their agents dominate the London salerooms. Although the 5th Earl of Rosebery (1847–1929), the 14th Earl of Moray (1816–1895), Sir Michael Shaw-Stewart, 7th baronet (1826–1903), and the 2nd Baron Leconfield (1830–1901) all made notable acquisitions, their overall contribution to the dispersal of the collection was comparatively modest. The most prolific buyer was an enigmatic banker called Christopher Beckett Denison (1823–1884), who acquired at least 284 lots at a hammer price of £50,000 as part of a campaign to furnish his newly acquired house on fashionable Upper Grosvenor Street, London.

The most significant purchases, however, were made by the Rothschilds. Seven members of the family from its British, French, German and Austrian branches are known to have spent in excess of £67,000 on thirty-seven lots. In Britain, Ferdinand de Rothschild (1839–1898) spent over £25,000 on fourteen lots, including furniture by Jean-Henri Riesener (now at Waddesdon Manor). His cousin, Alfred (1842–1918), had privately negotiated a remarkable pre-sale purchase of six items including a pair of candelabra attributed to Pierre Gouthière (now at the Huntington Library and Art Gallery, Pasadena), a clock signed by Jean-Antoine Lépine, and a lavish gold-mounted Byzantine sardonyx tazza (now at the National Museum of Scotland) – all for a staggering £24,000. The Rothschilds had already been a significant presence in the art market for several decades, but their prominence at the Hamilton Palace sale demonstrates the supremacy of the new plutocracy in the art market.

Rather more recent additions to the scene were the Americans who, in 1882, were just beginning to take their seats in the European salerooms. The banker Matthias Arnot (1833–1910) made the journey to London and bid in person on numerous paintings, finally securing eighteen works for his collection (now the Arnot Art Museum, New York). Most remarkable of all was the purchase made by William K. Vanderbilt (1849–1920), through the celebrated London dealers Samson Wertheimer and Frederick Davis, of arguably the two finest pieces of furniture in the sale: a lacquer commode and a secretaire made by Riesener for Marie Antoinette. For these two lots Vanderbilt paid a total hammer price of £18,900. They arrived in New York as the first acknowledged pieces of French royal furniture in the United States and set the scene for America's imminent dominance of the European art market.

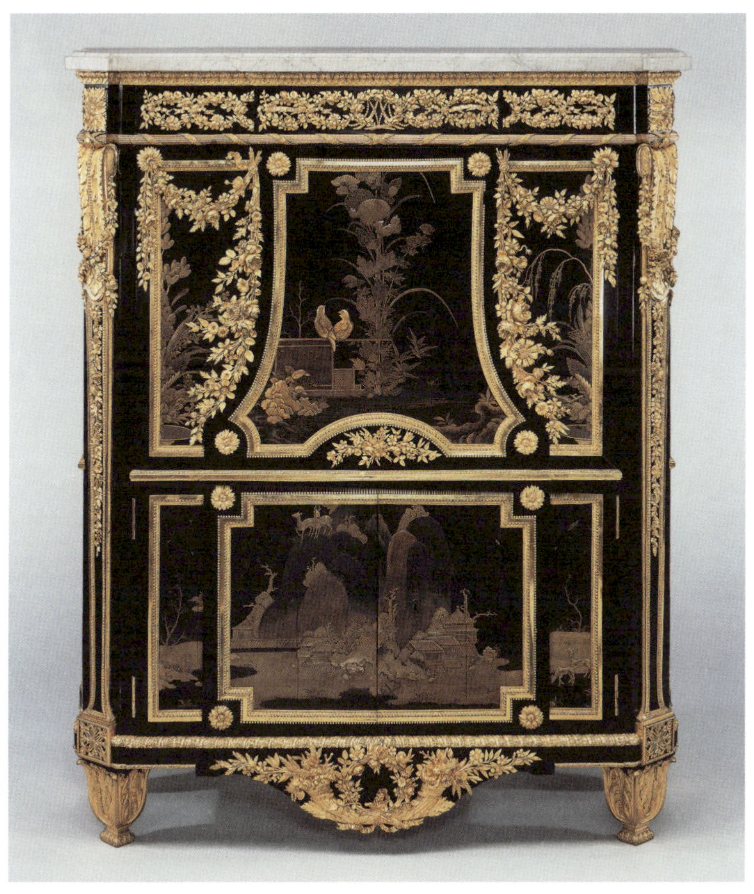

Jean-Henri Riesener, Secretaire, Paris, 1783, oak, ebony, other woods, Japanese lacquer, gilt-bronze, 144.8 × 109.2 × 40.6 cm, Metropolitan Museum of Art, New York

Yet the international reach of the Hamilton Palace sale did not just span the Atlantic; a selection of rather more modest items was acquired by the shipping magnate James Tannock Mackelvie (1824–1885) to form part of the founding collection of the Auckland Museum and Art Gallery in New Zealand.

Indeed, the growth of British public museums and art galleries in the mid-nineteenth century was also reflected in the demographic of the saleroom in 1882. The National Gallery spent almost £22,000 on thirteen paintings, and its director, Frederic Burton, was joined at Christie's by representatives from the National Portrait Gallery, London, the National Gallery of Ireland and the Department of Science and Art, which was then responsible for eponymous institutions in London (now the Victoria and Albert Museum), Edinburgh (now the National Museum of Scotland) and Ireland (now the National Museum of Ireland). The intense public interest in securing certain works for the national collections (saving them from foreign hands) was widely expressed in the national press – in stark contrast to previous generations, when the sale of a noble art collection had attracted popular interest principally on account of the scandalous details that brought it to pass.

The Hamilton Palace sale also serves to illustrate the growing professionalism and internationalism of the art trade. Art dealers were no longer mere merchants of bric-a-brac but were considered experts, connoisseurs and advisors. Their increasingly wealthy and international clientele raised the profile and dynamics of their profession. Their cluttered shops were becoming elegant showrooms with fashionable addresses, almost indistinguishable from the interiors their clients sought to create, and branches were established in cities on both sides of the Atlantic. In 1882 Joseph Duveen (1843–1908) was just starting out on his trajectory to international renown, purchasing thirteen lots from the Hamilton Palace sale for little over £1,000. By 1919, when the 13th Duke of Hamilton consigned the remaining contents of Hamilton Palace to Christie's, the firm of Duveen Brothers carried off the prize lot:

a portrait by George Romney of the Beckford children bought for
£54,600, which it then sold with more than a ten-thousand-pound profit to Henry E. Huntington (1850–1927), one of America's greatest industrialists and collectors.

The Hamilton Palace sale of 1882 reflects a seminal moment in the
history of the modern art market. By turning our gaze 180 degrees from
the contents of the sale to those who participated in its dispersal, we
gain a unique and full cast list of all the major protagonists in the art
market at the beginning of this vibrant period of world history. It might
rightly be considered the first sale of truly global consequence.

## 4   Berlin 1916–1932

In the final third of the nineteenth century, French Impressionists began to receive public recognition. Just a few years prior they had generally been regarded as maniacs who painted in a state of delirium tremens and had declared war on beauty.[76] Indeed, the Impressionists brought the art market into the modern era, not because of the high prices these works would achieve later but due to their initial lack of success. Traditional distribution channels were blocked as a result of general rejection, and the Impressionists needed to find sales alternatives. The solution was to sell through an art dealer (rather than directly to a client who commissioned the work). The lack of potential commissions meant that artists detached themselves from the taste of particular clients and began to define themselves as autonomous masters. The concepts of avant-garde as well as of artistic genius are rooted in this development. This also enhanced the prestige of the art dealer, since his own access to genius could be extended to others through the means of communication and interpretation.[77]

Around 1900 Paris was the centre for contemporary art. Apart from the leading dealer Paul Durand-Ruel there were initially just two galleries that also exhibited contemporary art: those of Ambroise Vollard and Berthe Weill.[78] In 1907 however, Daniel-Henry Kahnweiler opened his gallery. Raised in Stuttgart, he was friends with Pablo Picasso and Juan Gris, and the gallery quickly became the centre of a group of artists.

Through his contacts with dealers in London, Düsseldorf, and New York, Kahnweiler established his own network.[79] The first tough auction test for Impressionist art was the sale of Kahnweiler's private collection in Paris in 1921 to pay reparations. The first Picasso on the London market, a portrait, was sold at Christie's in 1937; it brought £157.[80]

One of the first successful dealers in contemporary art in Germany was Paul Cassirer (1871–1926). He was also secretary and later president of the Berlin Secession. In his Berlin art gallery he exhibited French Impressionists as well as works by Max Liebermann and Ernst Barlach.[81] In contrast to other more centralised European countries, contemporary art in Germany was distributed across several regional centres, such as Berlin, Munich, Dusseldorf, and Hamburg.

In those years the markets were however still dominated by Old Masters, and even more by the decorative arts.[82] Even in the 1920s the most expensive works on the market were not paintings, but objets d'art. In 1929 the most expensive picture sold at Christie's was a Van Dyck portrait for £17,850. In the same season, the firm reported sales of a fourteenth-century manuscript, the Luttrell Psalter, for £35,000, and of the celebrated Portland Vase for £30,450. Yet a watercolour by Paul Cézanne of Montagne Saint Victoire was sold at Sotheby's for just £400. The price of £1.4 million paid in the same year by Andrew Mellon for a group of twenty-one pictures from the St Petersburg Hermitage certainly does not reflect the commercial practice of the day, but rather the extraordinary circumstances of that particular museum sale.[83]

## 4 Paul Cassirer
## 81 Auctions between 1916 and 1932

From 1900 onwards, the Berlin metropolis grew into a centre for commerce and art that was unique in this period in Europe. The Paul Cassirer gallery exhibited works described as 'modern art', which at the time still referred to Impressionist and especially Post-Impressionist artists such as Paul Cézanne and Vincent van Gogh. Many small but notable collections were inspired by these exhibitions. It greatly annoyed the German Kaiser that the museum director Hugo von Tschudi purchased such works for the Neue Nationalgalerie in Berlin. However, in the summer of 1914 all this activity came to an abrupt halt, when a war began that would bring disaster on the world.

Paul Cassirer's business, which had been systematically importing art from France since its inception in 1898, now began to reverse its procedure, making a virtue of necessity. So far, the objective had been to sell art in Berlin. Now a way had to be found of reselling the art previously bought in Berlin. What could be better suited for this purpose than auctions?

To this end, Paul Cassirer entered into a partnership with his colleague Hugo Helbing from Munich. The first auction took place in the middle of the war, in the rooms of the Paul Cassirer gallery in Berlin on 22 May 1916. The collection to be sold was that of the recently deceased industrialist Julius Stern, and the top lot was Cézanne's *Red Tulips in a*

*Green Vase*, now in the Norton Simon Collection in Pasadena. The hammer price was 40,000 reichsmarks.

This was the first of eighty-one auctions organised by Paul Cassirer of Berlin and Hugo Helbing of Munich until October 1932. They usually offered one or more collections under the name of the owner and sold everything from paintings and drawings by old and new masters to sculpture, decorative arts and furniture.

The last auction sale during the First World War was auction no. 15, which took place on 11 November 1919. Auction no. 16 did not happen until five years later, on 15 December 1924. No auction sales took place in Germany during the time of inflation.

After Paul Cassirer's death in January 1926 my father, Walter Feilchenfeldt, managed the business. During the negotiations on war reparations, his successful dealings with the French contacts he had built in pre-war times had earned him a partnership in the firm. Under his leadership several great historic auction sales took place, in particular the Oscar Huldschinsky collection (auction no. 50, on 10 May 1928), the Joseph de Spiridon collection (auction no. 61, on 31 May 1929), and the Albert Figdor collection (auctions no. 72/73, on 11 June and 29 September 1930).

My father, who had previously been a publisher, was especially proud of the way the Oscar Huldschinsky collection was publicised. It was the first really great auction in Berlin. The firm sent out a bound catalogue with a white cover comprising 215 pages. All works were illustrated in copperplate, mostly on a full page. The book was 19 inches high, 13.9 inches wide and weighed 12.78 pounds. It became a collector's item, displayed on tables everywhere since no shelf was deep enough to take it, and it was retained because this luxurious object was too beautiful and valuable to be thrown out.

The marble hall of the hotel Esplanade was the setting for the auction of sixty-six paintings, forty sculptures and forty-one objects comprising English coloured engravings, miniatures, jewellery and silver, as well as a further eighty-eight lots listing gold boxes, furniture, textiles and more. The total result of the auction came to 4,167,370 reichsmarks. Huldschinsky was born in 1846 and had made his money among other investments in Upper Silesian steel works. His collection of Old Master paintings was of the finest quality and had been assembled from 1890 on the advice of the famous art historian Wilhelm von Bode.

The auction was a great success in every respect. The newspapers reported a result of 4.5 million reichsmarks. Among the sold lots was *Portrait of the painter Frans Post* by Frans Hals, purchased by a Berlin collector for 300,000 reichsmarks. Today it is in the Canadian National Gallery in Ottawa. Gabriel Metsu's *Sick Child* was bought for the Rijksmuseum in Amsterdam for 250,000 reichsmarks. The most expensive painting was Rembrandt's *Portrait of Hendrickje Stoffels* (570,000 reichsmarks), which was purchased by the London dealer Duveen Bros and is now in the Norton Simon Museum in Pasadena.

Towards the end of the year 1929, Black Thursday triggered the global economic crisis and a wave of bankruptcies and insolvencies that had never been seen before. In spite of this, Paul Cassirer held some more remarkable auction sales in Berlin, such as the Spiridon and Figdor collections already mentioned, which again took place in the hotel Esplanade's marble hall.

The sale of the Paris-based collection of Joseph de Spiridon was a particular coup for the new art market centre. There were again some spectacular successes: three panels from Sandro Botticelli's series *Nastagio degli Onesti* were bought by the dealership J & S Goldschmidt on behalf of the Prado in Madrid for 700,000 reichsmarks. Two paintings

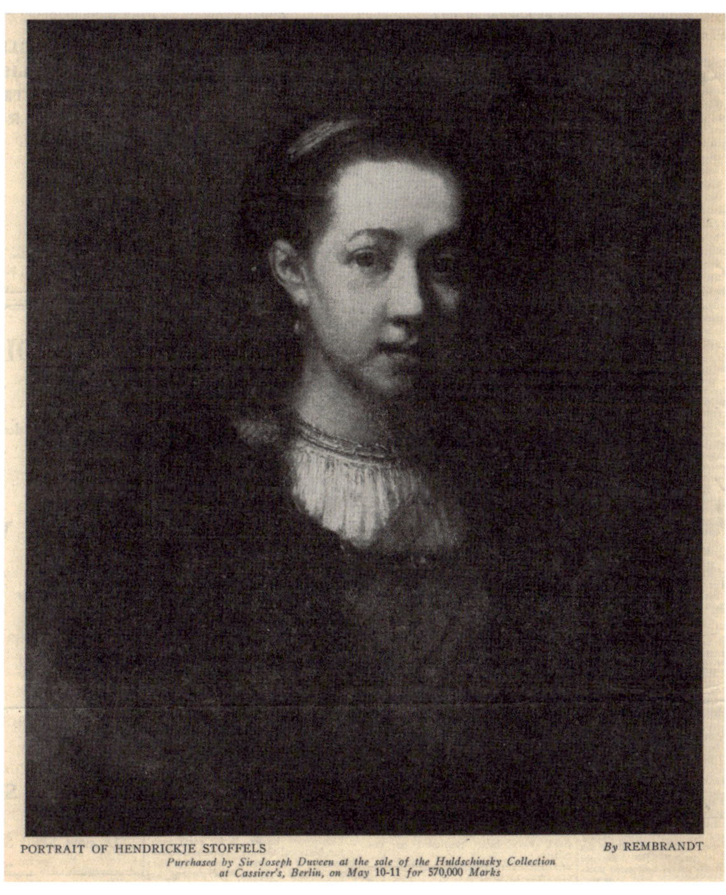



*The Art News*, Saturday, 9 June 1928, Paul Cassirer–Walter Feilchenfeldt Archive, Zurich

by Francesco Cossa depicting the saints Liberalis and Lucia were purchased by Duveen Bros for 750,000 reichsmarks. They resold them to the National Gallery in Washington.

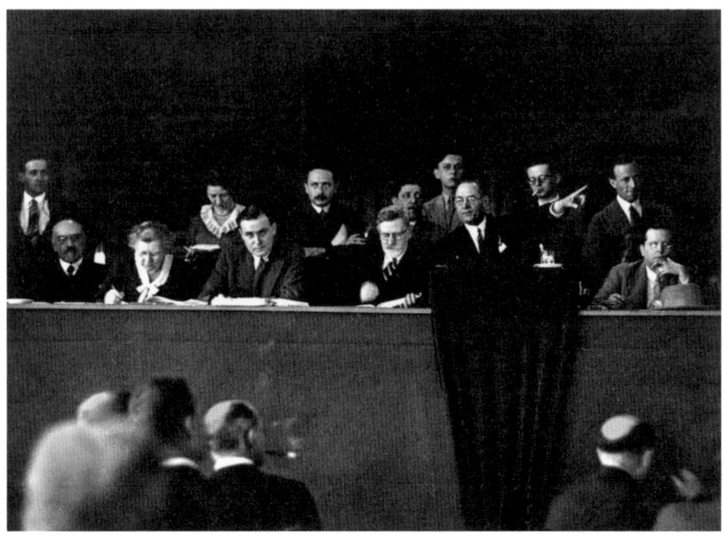

Figdor auction, 1930, Paul Cassirer–Walter Feilchenfeldt Archive, Zurich

It has been told that when the bids in the room dried up for Domenico Ghirlandaio's *Portrait of a Young Woman*, the auctioneer Hugo Helbing called out 'there is still time', which was an accepted practice for smaller objects and smaller sales, but in this case highly embarrassing, because he could have sold it at that point for a reduced commission. The painting was unsold and 'bought in', as recorded in the auctioneers book. However, my father was able to sell it after the auction to the famous Armenian collector Calouste Gulbenkian, and it is still in the Lisbon museum bearing his name today.

In 1930, the auction of the collection of the Viennese industrialist Albert Figdor was a joint enterprise with the Viennese fellow dealer Gustav Nebehay, who offered 810 lots of furniture and decorative art in

Vienna, while the paintings, sculptures, small boxes, bells, mortars, bronze objects, plaques and coats-of-arms were sold in Berlin. The Viennese section achieved a total of 5.2 million Austrian schillings, and the 572 lots in Berlin resulted in just below 3.9 million reichsmarks.

This collection was published over eight volumes. Volume 3 had an introductory essay by the editor, the art historian Max Friedländer, and listed 118 Old Master paintings by Italian, Dutch and Flemish, French, Spanish and German Schools. The firm of J. Goudstikker in Amsterdam bought *The Prodigal Son* by Hieronymus Bosch for 385,000 reichsmarks; today it is a highlight in the Boijmans van Beuningen museum in Rotterdam.

The last auction in Berlin was the only one conducted by my father himself, on 21 October 1932. To be sold was the estate of the artist Lesser Ury, comprising 129 oil paintings and 123 pastels. The total was 63,090 reichsmarks. My father used to recall his performance with delight, and maintained that auctioneering had been one of the most unforgettable, amusing and satisfying experiences of his career.

Walter Feilchenfeldt Senior took a leading role in two more auctions, but no longer under the banner of the firm of Paul Cassirer. Even at the beginning of the 1930s and thus before the National Socialists came to power in Germany, he tried to get a foothold in Paris and was, atypically, accepted by his French colleagues as a partner. On 9 June 1932, he was acting as expert specialist for the auctioneer Maître Alphonse Bellier in Paris for the sale 'S. &S. (Simon & Silberberg)'. Both collectors had been advised by him. The sale catalogue states: '*Experts Jos. Hessel et Etienne Bignou "Avec le concours de la maison Paul Cassirer de Berlin"*'. In contrast to Berlin, the Paris auctioneers and expert specialists were allowed to purchase lots in their own sales, which my father sadly did not have the wherewithal to do.

Out of thirty-one paintings and drawings, ten remained unsold, for example the Van Gogh drawing from the Silberberg collection, which was later seized by the National Socialists and housed in the East German Nationalgalerie in East Berlin until it was restituted to the Silberberg family after 1989 through the efforts of their lawyers. It was subsequently purchased by Ronald Lauder for the Museum of Modern Art in New York.

My father's last auction was the sale of the Margarete Oppenheim collection at the firm of Julius Böhler in Munich on 18 May 1936. This had a catastrophic result. Following 1,220 lots of decorative art, twelve paintings and watercolours were offered, among them nine by Cézanne. Only one sold.

Last but not least I would like to mention the auction 'Paintings and Sculptures by Modern Masters from German Museums' at Galerie Fischer in Lucerne on 30 June 1939. My father was in the saleroom, but he had asked all his friends to follow his example and refuse to bid. He did not believe in the legitimacy of this sale, neither from an ethical nor from a legal perspective. Two months later the Second World War started. One of its consequences among many was a lost decade for commerce.

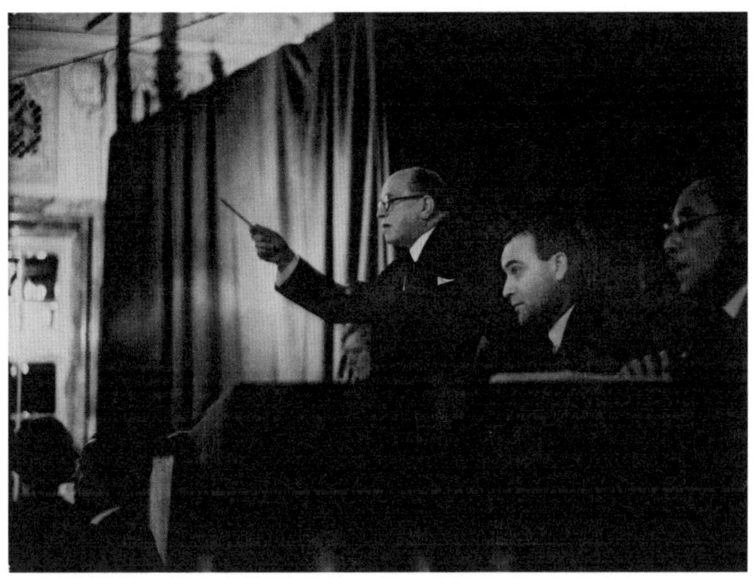

Spiridon auction, 1929, Paul Cassirer–Walter Feilchenfeldt Archive, Zurich

## 5  Lucerne 1939

The National Socialist regime had a far-reaching impact on all cultural activities, as well as on the art market. Creating a 'new German nation' involved purging, regulating and controlling cultural life. Any artists who were Jewish, or of Jewish descent, or who were 'Aryan' but whose work did not comply with the regime's 'blood and soil' ideology, were marked as 'degenerate' and were no longer allowed to practice. Undesirable museum directors, exhibition curators and university teachers were dismissed.[84] Anybody actively involved in cultural life, that is anybody working in the arts, music, film, radio, theatre, press, literature, architecture or the art trade, was forced to register in a state organisation, the so-called Reichskulturkammer, which had been founded in 1933. Only 'Aryan' Germans were permitted to do so, and membership was a prerequisite for any further employment. In addition, it made possible the surveillance of cultural actors.[85]

The extent of the exodus that followed these regulations is quite well known. It certainly brought about a great loss of expertise for art history and the art trade. At the same time, 'degenerate' works of art were removed from museums and collections, to be either destroyed as a public demonstration or to be sold abroad. The development culminated in the travelling exhibition *'Entartete Kunst'*, which opened in Munich in 1937. Simultaneously, the market for conformist art boomed; rising fear of impending war led to a rush towards tangible assets.[86]

The new cultural policy affected many Jewish private collections. As Jewish citizens had been excluded from economic and cultural life shortly after the Nazis seized power, many owners of art works were forced to sell these in order to finance their attempts to emigrate and start a new life abroad. After 1938, collections with Jewish owners were systematically plundered, even if they had been entrusted to state museums for safekeeping.[87] This was common practice not just in Nazi Germany but equally in all countries occupied by the Nazis.[88] After the occupation of France, Paris became the most important distribution centre for looted art in Europe.[89]

Switzerland, because it was neutral, was generally an important marketplace from 1933 to 1945.[90] This was also true for works of art. In 1996, in the wake of many headlines about 'Nazi Gold' in numbered bank accounts and an increasing awareness about looted art, a commission was founded to address the subject of Switzerland during the war: the Independent Commission of Experts Switzerland – Second World War (also known as the UAE for its German initials). The commission also shed light on the country's role in the trade of looted art. A report was published in 2001. The authors introduced a distinction between looted assets and 'flight assets', the latter referring to objects which were transferred by their owners to Switzerland and sold there. Title or restitution claims could only be brought for looted assets, which had been seized in areas under German occupation and then brought to Switzerland to be sold.[91]

## 5  The Antihero
## Theodor Fischer and the Auctioneer in the Age of Extremes

On 20 March 1939, 'degenerate' art works that had been removed from museums in the Third Reich and had been deemed unsellable were burned in the courtyard of the fire station at no. 42 Lindenstrasse in the Kreuzberg district of Berlin. Three months later, an international audience of museum curators, private collectors, art dealers and journalists gathered in Lucerne. At 3 p.m. Theodor Fischer began to auction 'Paintings and Sculptures by Modern Masters from German Museums'.[92]

The sale in Lucerne was a unique event in a double sense. On one hand, it was the only international auction of its kind involving works by the banned avant-garde. On the other hand, 'the Fischer sale' was subsequently viewed as a symbolic beacon of Modernism and came to embody the ideological battle waged by the National Socialist dictatorship against German art created before 1933.

Of the twenty thousand or so art works that had been removed from German museums from 1937 on, only a very small quantity was sold that day in Lucerne. Furthermore, out of a total of 125 lots, only eighty-five works sold. The proceeds of the auction however amounted to a disproportionately high percentage of the value of all art works sold by the Third Reich.[93] The five most expensive pictures in the sale, which included Vincent van Gogh's *Self-portrait* of 1888, constituted over half

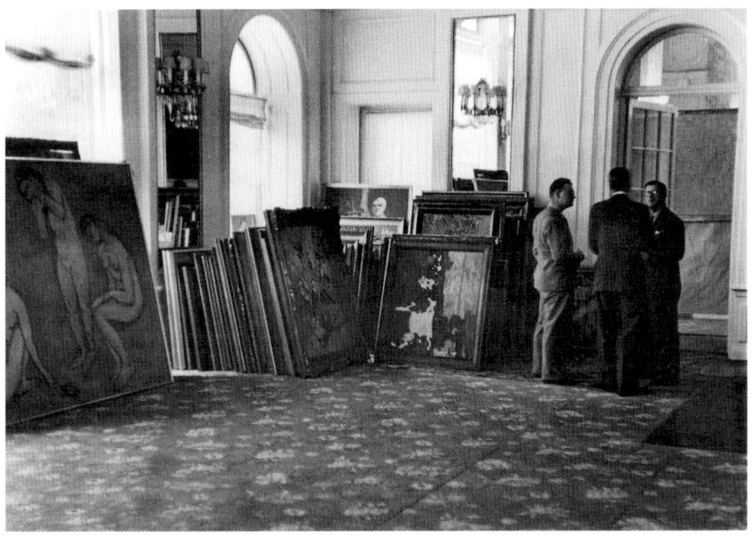

Preparations for the Galerie Fischer auction in the Grand Hotel National
in Lucerne, 1939, Galerie Fischer, Lucerne

the sale total. The majority of works were German, but the international works achieved higher sale rates and higher prices. German art from
late Impressionism to the Bauhaus school had not yet become an established part of the international market, so that their prices were mark-
edly lower than those paid for artists such as Van Gogh, Pablo Picasso,
or Henri Matisse.

In accordance with art auction practices, outstanding provenance
was utilised to maximise saleability. The museum provenance was
therefore not only mentioned in the sale title but was also listed in the
cataloguing of each work. The works, moreover, were not belittled, as
they had been for example in the wall texts for the '*Entartete Kunst*' (degenerate art) exhibition held in Munich in 1937. Had any attempt been

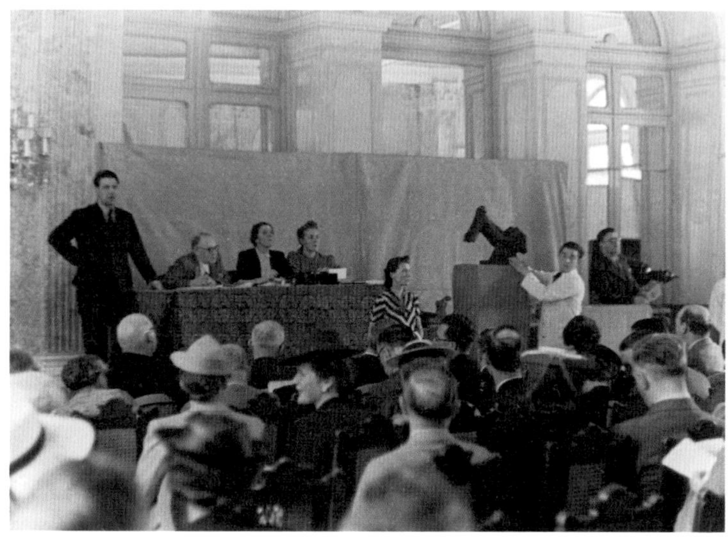

Sale of Ernst Barlach's sculpture *Der Rächer* (The avenger) on 30 June 1939, with
Theodor Fischer on the rostrum at the far left, source: Galerie Fischer, Lucerne

made to conceal the origins of the prominent works, this would probably have further intensified the criticism that was already being levelled
at the event. While the German side had intended to use the sale as a
'test run' to explore the potential for further international sales, the
outbreak of war impeded a further attempt to auction off a selection of
prints.[94]

The potential buyers came from a relatively limited group of museums and private collectors in Europe and North America. Many of
these however refused to bid in order to protest what was clearly a blatant attempt by the Germans to procure foreign currency. Bids were
taken in Swiss francs. Once he had deducted his costs, Theodor Fischer
transferred the proceeds in pound sterling to a London account. As

critics had suspected, the entire sale profits went towards the German war effort, while the affected museums were compensated only partly and at minimum.

The Fischer sale established – under very dubious circumstances – the very first international auction results for works of classic German Modernism. Critics opposed it as collaboration with the regime (albeit indirect). For their part, buyers claimed that they were coming to the rescue of modern art– a speculative but plausible argument, considering what proved to be a frenzy of destruction on the part of the German government. The same excuse was cited after the war by art dealers who had been involved in the exploitation. The entire 'degenerate art' initiative was limited in both time and scope, but its damage to the German museum community was all the greater. Paradoxically, the Lucerne sale and the individual sales from 1938 to 1941 achieved the exact opposite of the ministry of propaganda's intent: very little foreign currency came in, but the ideologically poisoned act of de-accessioning museum works heightened the international recognition and dissemination of 'degenerate' art works.

The auctioneer Theodor Fischer earned his commission from the sale, and he also benefited from both international attention and continuous business contacts as an art dealer with the Third Reich and its art agents up to the end of the war. Fischer was not at all dependent on the German government however. Conducting the sale in 1939 was therefore an act of opportunism, and it helped establish Switzerland as a marketplace for the international art trade, together with the so-called 'emigrant auctions' that Fischer also conducted. As the biggest local firm, Fischer's was uniquely positioned to auction large mixed-category collections. In addition, Fischer had an international clientele.[95]

The debate surrounding the moral implications of the Lucerne sale is symptomatic of the radical changes the profession of the auctioneer underwent during the 'age of extremes.' (The term is Eric Hobsbawm's.) In the course of just a few years, neutral agents for the procurement of art and cultural goods became active participants in a market determined by National Socialist cultural and racial policies. The example of the Third Reich demonstrates a reorientation of the art trade profoundly shaped by ideology, which had consequences not just for the art market but also for its personnel structure, supply and distribution channels.

Art dealers and auctioneers who had previously been relatively independent were now subject to a system of rigid political and economic control exerted by the Reichskulturkammer (the Reich chamber of culture), a subdivision of the ministry for propaganda and public enlightenment led by Joseph Goebbels).[96] When studied thoroughly in the late 1990s, the Reichskammer der bildenden künste (Reich authority for the fine arts) was found to have successively exerted pressure to conform (*gleichschaltung*) on the art trade and especially the auction business.[97] Every administrative step in the auction process was determined by this art trade agency, which also had the central task of eliminating all members deemed Jewish under the Nuremberg Laws.

Loss of Reichskammer membership was synonymous with loss of livelihood – hence the withdrawal and emigration of the important art dealers and auctioneers of the pre-1933 period, and the establishment of new companies, be it through 'Aryanization' or founding new ones. This profound shift in the art market occurred from Berlin and Munich to Frankfurt am Main and Vienna (after the 1938 annexation of Austria) as well as in all occupied countries.[98] Well-established firms were replaced by new protagonists, significant dealerships such as A.S. Drey

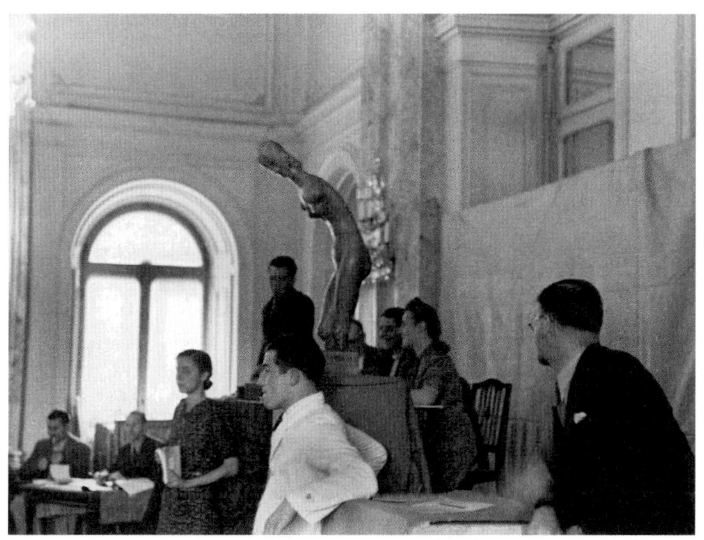

Sale of a sculpture by Wilhelm Lehmbruck on 30 June 1939,
source: Galerie Fischer, Lucerne

found themselves forced to liquidate their stock, while 'Aryan' auctioneers not only sold their very stock but also the businesses of former
German citizens who were obliged to liquidate their property under
the anti-Semitic laws.

For the art trade and private collectors this was the end of an era.
During the Nazi period the old elite, insofar as it was Jewish, was replaced with a new one that bought predominantly at auction, as recent
research demonstrates.[99] The complete exclusion of Jewish auctioneers
from the German art trade in the period until 1938 is well documented.
From 1935–37 there was a significant increase in new companies, in
particular auction houses, including firms selling important collections
as well as local companies specializing in household liquidations. Before

this an auctioneer could claim to be a neutral agent between consignor and buyer, but under the Nazi dictatorship this impartiality could not be maintained.

Voluntarily or involuntarily, the auctioneer became the henchman of the regime. The so-called 'Jew Auctions', which disposed of art and cultural possessions from Jewish private collections, demonstrate a reinterpretation of language typical for the Third Reich. Traditional terms such as 'voluntary auction sale' were turned on their heads.

Even the terminology of the art auction reflected the shift in social norms, as the auctioneers did not hesitate to make use of the good name and reputation of collectors (and dealers) to increase the value of many important auction sales. The dissolution of the Margraf company in Berlin is one such example. Another was the sale of the estate of the Hamburg collector Emma Budge. Such prominent sales were guaranteed to attract buyers' interest. A vast supply of art works now flooded an increasingly isolated market. (The German art market had become purely domestic with the start of the war.) The demand rose with each year of the war, and prices rose with it; attempts by the government to end or at least regulate the 'flight to tangible assets' were in vain.[100]

The majority of collections were sold anonymously, however. For the most part, this *damnatio memoriae* instigated by the Nazi state succeeded – until very recently. Names and biographies of pre-war collectors, dealers and auctioneers were relegated to oblivion, or remained known only to specialist art historians. Conversely, the new entrepreneurs benefited not just from these cataclysmic changes but also from continuities in the art world that extended into the post-war period and beyond.[101] Compliance with the Nazi system was downplayed as a mere 'service'.[102]

Nazi era auction catalogues – with their handsome craftsmanship, multiple images, provenance, literature and exhibition listings, and sometimes even with prefaces written by distinguished German museum experts who had assisted the auction house in the cataloguing work – illustrate the seamless integration of what are essentially documents of loss and displacement into the pseudo-legal Nazi system of injustice. Today, these catalogues are valuable sources for provenance research following the 1998 Washington Conference Principles on Nazi-Confiscated Art. Even at the time they were created, these publications made it clear when 'non-Aryan' goods were being sold; a 1938 Nazi law (the so-called *Tarnverordnung*) prohibited 'Jewish' businesses and individuals from 'camouflaging' their assets.[103] An art work, in other words, could not officially be liquidated without the object's 'Jewish' ownership first being acknowledged.

This new research has made it possible once again to bring buried biographies to light and to compile, in small steps, a revised history of the art and auction market in the twentieth century.

## 6  Stuttgart 1947–1962

After the Second World War, the contemporary art trade in Germany faced a late and painfully slow restart. Innumerable artists and dealers had emigrated between 1933 and 1945. Nevertheless, private galleries began to open even in the late 1940s, and even more so in the 1950s, in particular in the Rhineland.[104] The economic upswing in the area contributed to this development. The most significant auctions at the time with regard to promoting the modern art that had been vilified during the Third Reich were held at the Stuttgarter Kunstkabinett. Between 1947 and 1962, its owner, Roman Norbert Ketterer, who was also the executor for the estate of Ernst Ludwig Kirchner, sold German Expressionist art.[105]

During this time, the gallery became an established centre for dealing in contemporary art as well as a social gathering point. The high quality of its exhibitions, the attention they attracted from the (international) public, and last but not least its network of connections leading to purchases by state museums all played a part. Previews became compulsory events for those who perceived themselves as part of a cosmopolitan elite. The first contemporary art fair took place in Lausanne in 1965, driven by the need of gallery owners for professional co-operation and co-ordination. Inspired by its success, the German exhibitors Hein Stünke and Rudolf Zwirner organised the first German contemporary art fair, known as the Kölner Kunstmarkt (today Art

Cologne).[106] Since Cologne was regarded as the secret capital of the German art trade, the Cologne Art Market was intended to counterbalance the fact that Germany, unlike its neighbouring countries, did not have a national art metropolis.[107]

In 1955 the first documenta took place in Kassel. Originally it had been conceived to reconnect modern art with the public after the 'dark years' of National Socialisism, but over the years it developed into the biggest exhibition of contemporary art worldwide.[108] The art market did not only benefit from the exposure of a wider public to modern art. For any works on view, the documenta functioned as a stepping stone on the way to a museum exhibition, which continues to have at least a temporary effect on the price level for works by contributing artists.[109] For the first time, contributing artists also created works that the organisers then sold as an edition. This was introduced first for the documenta 3 in 1964, and met with harsh criticism because of the merging of art and commerce. Seen against the background of today's commercial marketing activities in museums, the initiative appears progressive.

Demand on the secondary market was initially hampered by a lack of liquidity. The general preference was still for decorative art more than for traditional painting, even though the 1950s saw a renewed interest in Old Masters. The preference had practical reasons; many collectors were replacing any war losses in their inventory, not only driven by a love for antiquities but also by a lack of availability for contemporary products.[110] The price increase in the decorative arts during the 1950s was significantly above that of traditional painting and was led by works by eighteenth-century French cabinet-makers. For the first time, there was a wider awareness of art as investment; and for the first time at the end of the 1950s the returns outperformed those for equity, gold and other asset classes.[111]

# 6 Roman Norbert Ketterer, or the Return of Expressionism

The gathering on a cool May morning reminds me of an alumni meeting at a rather posh university (family members welcome). The gentlemen bustling about on the steps outside have the distinguished features of avant-garde film protagonists, and their suits are of an elegance that transcends any crumpling. A little tweed, some flannel.... We imagine that any wallets in the inside pockets would not have to be bulging, since the pockets as such are bound to be deep.[112]

Thus wrote the columnist 'Sybille', wife of a Munich publisher, who never hid her affiliation with the same social class she commented on. With fluent charm she delivered the portrait of a man who for years provoked discussions as well as provided a prime contact in the art world: Roman Norbert Ketterer, self-made man and auctioneer. He was clearly a product of the embryonic emergence of the Federal Republic of Germany. He maintained that he never had a mentor, let alone an education in art history. Instead, in a very short time he attracted not just the obligatory portion of envy and criticism but also a clientele made up of the country's foremost industrialists, collectors, and museum curators. He also shared a common goal with these prominent figures: to renew the appeal of German Expressionist art, whose creators had been persecuted by the Nazis and whose works had been banned, removed from museums and destroyed. This was a highly attractive undertaking at the time, and not just in the then comparatively inartistic environment of Stuttgart. There should be an art market again – and provenance was of no concern.

Ketterer was a native of the Baden region and would have become a missionary had his provincial schoolmasters had their way. As a practitioner of the art trade, he soon took over a leading role, and over fifteen years delivered auctions at a level that, to some of his clients, seemed to resemble a flamboyant circus act rather than the result of actual hard work. From 1947 to 1962 he held thirty-seven sales in Stuttgart at an ever-grander series of venues. Since the war, this was for many their first encounter with a wealth of modern art, especially as even museum employees only knew *'die Moderne'* from reproductions. At the same time, the Ketterer firm, as well as the art market in general, could register superlative price rises in the 1950s.

According to Sybille, 'he managed to drive up German Expressionist art as if it were the Mercedes share price. He can now boast of around thirty-five auctions, a title story in *Spiegel* magazine, and a turnover in the millions. He is en vogue. He is the person to go to: the Dior of auctioneering.'[113]

The rediscovery of a Modernism believed to have been lost was also the recovery of a market without boundaries for those early twentieth-century German drawings, watercolours and paintings that had survived the Third Reich and the war. After the country's *Stunde Null* – its zero hour – as the economy grew under new conditions and after the currency reform of 1948, auctions became more and more international. Private collections that had survived were dispersed, not least due to financial considerations, while new ones formed; the art trade was open for business; museums began operating and organizing exhibitions again.

It seems almost as if the museums tried to prove to the international community that Germany too had had a modern art movement, even though this view did not always have the full support of their own ranks. Werner Doede, director of the Düsseldorf Kunstsammlungen, commented critically in a 1985 interview on the attitude of some former colleagues: 'While I tried to rebuild the much decimated department of modern art, which had been subject to severe losses in the 1937 confiscations of "degenerate art", I was sometimes condescendingly told that, well, those Munich exhibitions, that was really the only sensible thing the Nazis ever did. ... This remained the prevailing view for a long time, and I was criticised behind my back.'[114]

In spite of such discord, museums tried to counteract the past, investing their small budgets in special exhibitions and buying 'replacement' works for Expressionist art that had been confiscated by the Nazis. Just a few years earlier, nobody would have thought such attempts at compensation possible – certainly not Roman Norbert Ketterer from Bräunlingen, the man for small and large deals who had started out in the 1930 at an oil company in Eislingen. The firm was later deemed to be of military importance, which is why he did not have to join the army. Even after the foundation of the Stuttgarter Kunstkabinett in 1946 Ketterer kept a foothold in the oil business; in addition he was adroit in local politics in his home region of Baden-Wurttemberg and maintained good relations with the American military government.

Not surprisingly in November 1945 the local Kommandatur in Göppingen granted him a rather diffuse license for 'wholesale in all kinds of works of art'. 'Since I did not know with what kind of art I would concern myself, I refrained from using the term "gallery"', he recalled.'[115]

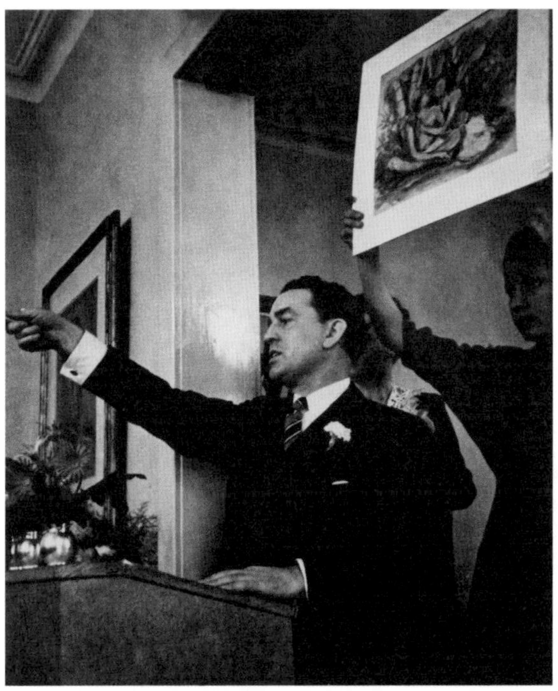

Roman Norbert Ketterer at the Stuttgarter Kunstkabinett's
second auction, which took place on 26–27 February, 1948,
at no. 65 Eberhardstrasse in Stuttgart

Ketterer was now free to take up any form of art trade. He chose auctions,
with his headquarters in southern Germany. This also had political
benefits, since the American and French military administration were
the most favourably inclined among the four occupying powers to fos-
tering the general cultural climate through, for example, exhibition
projects. The post-war concept of 're-education' was partly based on the
conviction that modern art and democratic principles were inherently

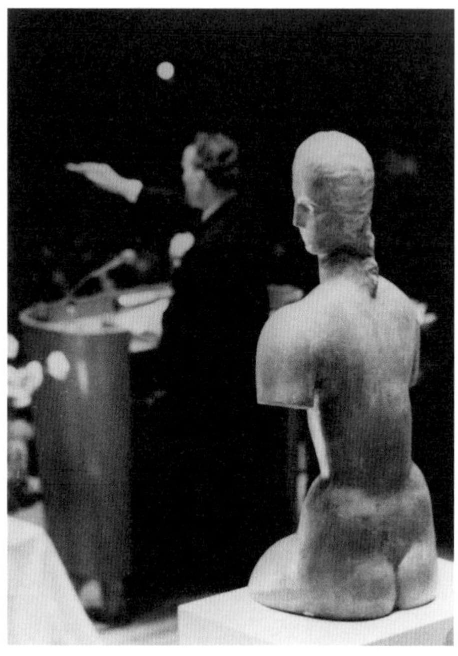

Auction in May 1961 in the studio of the Süddeut-
scher Rundfunk Stuttgart in Villa Berg (with a
female torso by Wilhelm Lehmbruck in the fore-
ground)

connected. The first documenta exhibition in Kassel was a project un-
dertaken in the same vein.[116]

Ketterer was in his mid thirties when he decided to focus his ener-
gies on the fine arts and discover German Expressionism for himself.
In this he was well advised by private collectors and museum curators.
He began to travel constantly to acquire consignments, criss-crossing
the federal states of West Germany, moving into Berlin via the Airlift,
and finally arriving in the United States in the 1950s. An early contact

he made during his extensive search for heirs, dealers and emigrants was the publisher Henri Nannen, another dynamic young man. Years later, Nannen recalled the fledgling art dealer: 'He had dark curls and a chiselled Roman profile, and he was full of energy.'[117] Nannen had the artist contacts, while Ketterer owned a car, which proved useful for art transport and visiting artists. One of them founded newspapers, invented the successful magazine *Stern* and in his later years collected and dealt in German Expressionists, and finally established a museum in his home town of Emden. The other one reinvented himself, went to Stuttgart, set up the eponymous Stuttgarter Kunstkabinett Moderne Kunst, and became the most successful auctioneer in early post-war Germany.

When she was 73 years old, Marianne Feilchenfeldt gave her personal summary during a conversation with her fellow art dealer Ketterer, himself not much her junior: 'You had a certain charm from your native Baden, and this took the edge off the usual deadly seriousness, which was definitely part of your success. God only knows where you managed to find all those art works. You were a jolly young man with a carnation in your lapel, and you took the sales with a natural insouciance. I would say your boldness was always attractive.'[118] We owe the quotation from the Zurich art dealer, as well as many others in this essay, to Ketterer's large scale 'late work', published in two volumes in 1988. This memorable self-portrait with guest appearances contained 952 pages of richly illustrated 'dialogues' about art, the art trade and Ketterer auctions after 1945. It is an amazing kaleidoscope of eyewitness accounts and art world news.

The first auction of the Stuttgarter Kunstkabinett took place from 2 to 4 September 1947 in the not particularly glamourous rooms of the carpet dealer Emil Meyer.

Only the final section listed prints by the artists whose names were to become the main repertory in the years to come: Ernst Barlach, Max Beckmann, Oskar Kokoschka, Lyonel Feininger, and the Brücke artists. The currency of this first sale was still reichsmarks, and the engraving *Hier ist Geist* by Beckmann went durig the auction from 180 up to 410 reichsmarks. However, when the fourth auction took place a few months after the currency reform of September 1948, 'nobody quite knew what prices were right', as Ketterer recalled in his memoirs. 'I started Max Beckmann's *Selbstbildnis mit steifem Hut* at 20 deutschmarks (the estimate was 40 deutschmarks), and there was no bid. Then Herr Burmeister, representing the Hamburg-based trade firm Commeter, bid 18 marks.'[119]

Günter Busch, who was director of the Kunsthalle Bremen until 1983, also used Beckmann as an example for the potential of those years; the museum had lost all but a few of its Beckmann prints through Nazi confiscation. In the 1980s the collection was once again complete, due to the affordability of the works. He began to buy in 1948, when prices were around 30 marks, and they remained stable until the 1950s. 'Then they went up to 50 to 120 marks. Because we lacked funds for the museum, I said to myself at the time: you can buy German Expressionists cheaper than [Paul] Klee or [Franz] Marc. . . .'

Watercolours by Emil Nolde were on a different trajectory and were popular, especially with the ladies in the saleroom. The art historian Horst Keller, who later became director of the museum in Cologne, supplied a cheerful commentary about the 'special Nolde watercolour festival' at Ketterer's:

> Now safer than stocks and shares . . . the very colours of drowning landscapes appeal to the private buyer. And then the flowers! Vine leaves and dahlias . . . rose to 13,000 marks. The

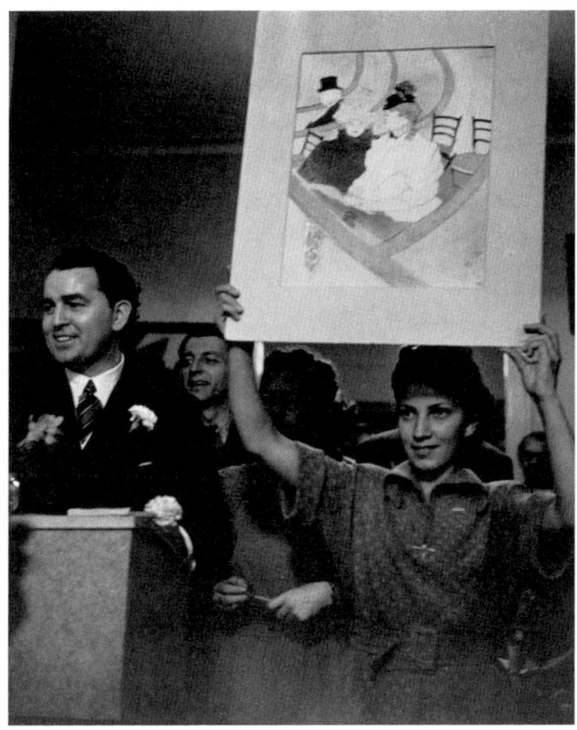

Ketterer and his employee Elsbeth Stoiber during the Kunstkabinett's sixth auction, on 26–28 October, 1949 (with the lithograph *La grande loge* by Henri de Toulouse-Lautrec from the Gerstenberg collection)

absolute record for a Nolde watercolour on the very wide horizon of art was however Lot 662: Dahlias and Sunflowers = 18,000 marks (five years ago this would have bought 18 of them). Flowers by [Max] Pechstein, flowers by Christian Rohlfs, flowers even by [Karl] Schmidt-Rottluff: no end to hands being raised.[120]

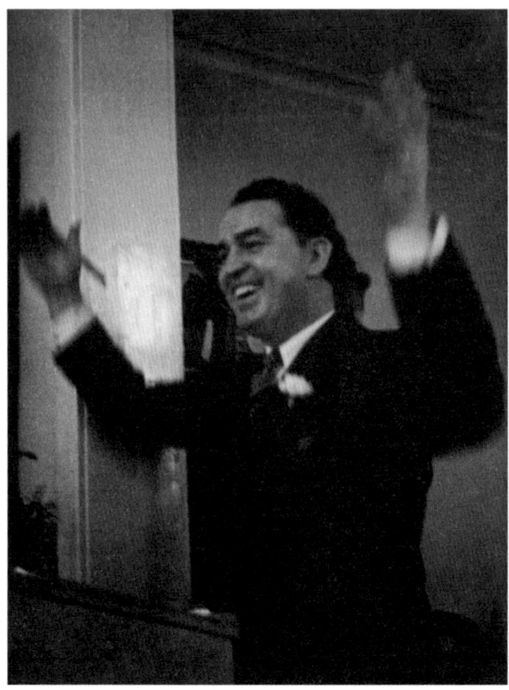

Roman Norbert Ketterer in the auction room on Eberhardstrasse in Stuttgart, circa 1948

A 'festival of buoyant prices', was Keller's conclusion, while he did not fail to add that Picasso works on paper had held up well, too. 'If you are concerned about modern art not really being a topic of conversation, the experience in Stuttgart will make you think better of it.'[121]

It soon got around that the prices for paintings in those years were out of reach for most museum directors; they competed unsuccessfully against young and moneyed collectors. In the late 1950s Ketterer could announce record prices at regular six-month intervals. A work by Wassily Kandinsky made 118,000, estimated at 75,000 marks! Sensational prices for Paul Klee! Half a million for a collection of Feiningers! Prices finally went through the roof at the thirty-seventh auction in May 1962, when *Overgrown House* by Edvard Munch sold for 210,000 marks. It had been consigned from Argentina and went to the Munch Museum in Oslo. The total was 8.5 million marks for 1,103 lots, of which only five remained unsold. Nobody expected this to be the last sale.

Ketterer had turned over millions and supplied entire collections, he had advised Hans Heinrich von Thyssen-Bornemisza on acquisitions for his collection, and he had shipped art works and documentation for Will Grohmann across the military zones to Stuttgart. When Ketterer announced the sale of the collection of Nell Walden, formerly in the possession of the *Sturm* art magazine editor Herwarth Walden, the public was dumbstruck, while the press called the auction the most important sale in post-war West Germany.

Sometime around 1960, Ketterer seems to have explored new avenues. The temptation to concentrate on contemporary art was considerable – and to compete with the capital cities of the art trade. At this point, 'collectors and artist heirs were still willing to sell art works, as the economy just about held up', wrote the art critic Erhard Göpel as prices levelled out.[122] But he feared that worse was to come.

Roman Norbert Ketterer left the economic conditions and its vagaries behind. Convinced that he had reached the pinnacle of his career as an art dealer, he closed his firm and moved to the Swiss enclave of Campione in Ticino. The Swiss print dealer Hans Bolliger could not believe 'that the great adversary should suddenly withdraw, without having died or gone bankrupt, or for any other obvious reasons'.[123]

# 7    Bern 1951

For a large part of the art market, the recession of the 1930s continued until the end of the Second World War.[124] The war had two significant consequences. London was strengthened as a marketplace while its competitor Paris was occupied by the German army. And New York became the centre for contemporary art, replacing Paris as the home of the avant-garde, since important artists had emigrated there.[125] Many galleries were founded, with Leo Castelli's probably being the most famous; he represented a large number of major contemporary artists, including Robert Rauschenberg, Jasper Johns, Frank Stella, Cy Twombly and Roy Lichtenstein. The cultural elite of Western industrialised countries began to travel to New York to stay informed about new developments. Conversely, traces of the 'American way of life' could now be found all over Europe, first because of the post-war occupation, and later because of far-reaching trade relations. This was especially true for Switzerland; sizeable American cars could be seen on the streets of Zurich, while Swiss collectors and museum directors visited New York galleries.

The national art market soon began to respond with demand for international works of art, in addition to the clearly defined 'Swiss art'. Ferdinand Hodler, the brothers Giovanni and Augusto Giacometti and their cousins, the brothers Alberto and Diego Giacometti, as well as Jean Tinguely heralded the country's entry into Modernism. Long before the international auction houses arrived, auctions were held by medium-sized enterprises. The most important firms for fine art auctions were certainly Fischer in Lucerne, long established since 1907, and its competitors H. G. Gutekunst, founded in Stuttgart in 1846 and from 1919 based in Berne. From 1960, the Zurich firm Koller became the first port of call for applied arts and Old Masters, with a wide range of offers and a variable volume of sales.[126] Another general provider was Galerie Dobiaschofsky in Berne, established as a gallery in 1923; the founder's son added auctions to its portfolio in 1959.

Similar to most other European states, Switzerland had no regulations restricting cross-border trade, but because of the economic situation it became a major transit country and trading centre for art.[127] After the war, auction sales first fell under regulations that also applied to travelling salesmen and door-to-door peddlers. Regulations specific to the procedures applied to voluntary public auction sales were only established in 1979.[128]

Since the mid-twentieth century, Switzerland's most important role has been perhaps that of an interim storage site for art.[129] The free ports in Zurich, Geneva, Basel and Chiasso have specialised in warehousing art works for foreign owners. There is no import tax levied on objects in such storage. These sites are a great advantage in particular to the cross-border art trade, since a work can be exported from the country of sale and then exported into the country where the purchaser resides. The same applies to works that are stored for investment purposes. The free ports have traditionally been actual service centres with restorer's workshops, but also with galleries to sell the works which were brought in.[130]

## 7 Eberhard Kornfeld
## Connoisseurship and Tradition

In 2014, Galerie Kornfeld celebrates its sesquicentennial. H.G. Gutekunst founded his gallery for old and modern art in Stuttgart in 1864. Five generations have led the company since then, with each contributing in its own way to tradition and introducing new artistic and commercial elements. Eberhard W. Kornfeld (since 1951) and Christine E. Stauffer (since 1967) shape the firm with the gallery's new partner Bernhard U. Bischoff (since 2014) and with the support of art historians Simon Oberholzer, Lea Raffl, and Patricia Schmidinger. The financial side is handled by Jörg and Christoph Kunz. Compared to all other auction houses, this is a small but efficient team.

Kornfeld, born in Basel in 1923, began to work at Gutekunst & Klipstein in 1945. August Klipstein (1885–1951) died unexpectedly in April 1951. The director of the Basel Kunstmuseum Georg Schmidt wrote in his obituary: 'When August Klipstein opened one of his famous auctions, private print collectors, museum curators and art dealers from far and wide sat at his feet like a large family gathered around a revered and awe-inspiring fatherly friend. Expectations were not just of a mere business transaction but of an entertaining as well as artistic experience.' Ferdinand Möller sent his condolences from Cologne on 9 April 1951: 'I am very distressed by Dr Klipstein's death. I wish to offer you and the entire team my heartfelt condolences. The passing away of this venerable

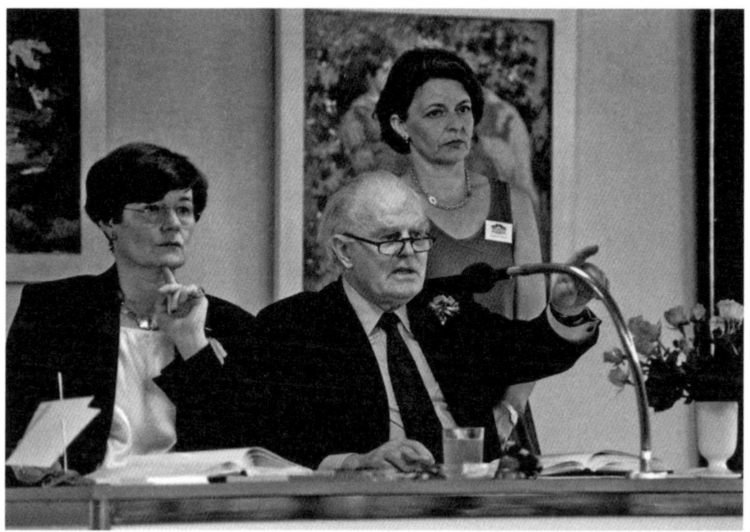

Eberhard Kornfeld and Christine Stauffer on the rostrum

colleague will leave a large gap for all of us. Over many decades, in times of war and peace, he was a saviour for many; he will never be forgotten.' To replace a personality of this stature was a considerable challenge for the twenty-eight-year-old Kornfeld. He mastered it in Klipstein's own spirit: 'Primary objective: to deliver sterling quality work in the service of art, and to be committed to the benefit of the company with one's entire strength.' The difference with the auction houses in Paris, London and New York, who were already world market leaders at the time, begins here. Kornfeld shaped an atmosphere that distinguishes his auction house to this day!

From 1955, the style of the auction catalogues changed. There were no longer brief factual details but instead extensive articles containing the results of original research, quotations and above all detailed infor-

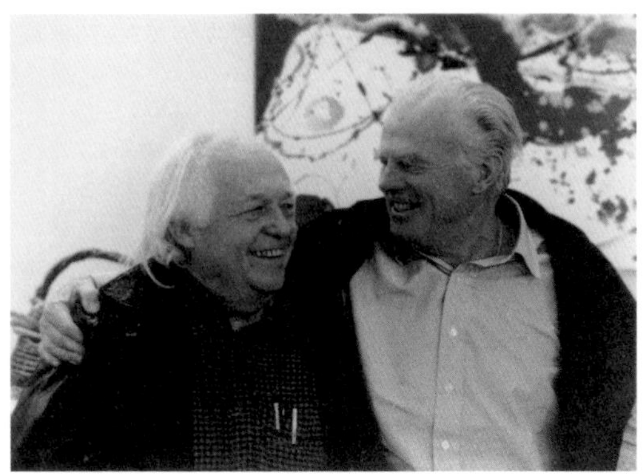

Sam Francis and Eberhard Kornfeld

mation on the provenance of each work. Over time, the catalogues became sought-after reference books, comparable only to C.G. Boerner's stock catalogues from Düsseldorf. The involvement of Hans Bolliger (1915–2002) led to specialist book auctions in the 1960s, and his catalogues *Dokumentationsbibliothek I–V* remain indispensable for experts to this day.

In order to have more time for art historical and other research (the firm's library is one of the largest in the international art trade), training, and client service, Kornfeld decided already in 1960 to reduce his auctions to one series per year. The supply of the very finest art works, moreover, continued to decline. This concept was unthinkable to the competition, which instead responded to the booming art market by expanding and continually developing new collecting areas and markets.

In 1970, Traudl Bruckner and Ernst Beyeler approached Kornfeld with the idea of creating an art fair in Basel, which could possibly coincide with his auctions. Art Basel and Kornfeld's auctions still take place at the same time.

The art market is on an ever-accelerating trajectory, and an enthusiastic media accompanies it every step of the way. The number of annual art fairs worldwide has increased to about fifty today, while the number of auctions has become virtually incalculable. Kornfeld remains unruffled, but he also responds to the demands of the market. His sale catalogues went online in 2006. In 2008 he reluctantly began to accept bids by telephone. For him, a *work of art* remains a *work of art*. It is certainly not regarded as *sale material* as it is termed in so many other auction houses.

It would be remiss not to mention the auction dinners. After days of battling each other in the saleroom, a complete change of scene occurs in the evening in the ballroom of the Bellevue Hotel, and all the competitors sit peacefully together in one festive art trade family.

Apart from annual auctions, individual exhibitions regularly take place at the gallery, usually featuring contemporary artists. Good examples for continuity in this area are a constant dedication to the work of Pablo Picasso, Marc Chagall, Alberto Giacometti and Sam Francis, with whom Kornfeld has maintained a lifelong friendship and some of whose prints he published from 1961. In this context, the sensational 1964 publication of *One Cent Life* by Sam Francis must be mentioned: the first comprehensively illustrated book with original lithographs by almost all the representatives of Pop Art. In 1970 Kornfeld founded a branch in Zurich led initially by Christoph Albertini, in addition to the office in Bern. A number of important exhibitions are shown there, frequently by Swiss artists.

Kornfeld also continues to build on August Klipstein's scholarly work. He published the catalogue raisonné of prints by Käthe Kollwitz, based on Klipstein's initial research, in 1955, followed by catalogues raisonnés of prints by Paul Klee in 1963 and Marc Chagall in 1966. Paul Signac and Paul Gauguin followed. In close co-operation with the authors Kornfeld published the catalogues raisonnés of Max Beckmann paintings and Picasso's prints (in seven volumes) as well as a new edition of the Kollwitz catalogue raisonné. In addition to a comprehensive biography of Ernst Ludwig Kirchner he is now publishing Kirchner's graphic oeuvre and is working on the catalogue raisonné of prints by Alberto Giacometti. These publications form an indispensable basis for all collectors, galleries, museums and auction houses. No other art dealer worldwide can demonstrate this level of scholarly activity in the field of prints.

For his eightieth birthday, Christine Stauffer edited a commemorative publication in his honour. International and renowned art historians contributed fifty-one essays to celebrate the life and work of the man as well as the auctioneer, art dealer, publisher and collector. The University of Bern awarded him an honorary doctorate for his research already in 1982. In 1984 he was awarded the prestigious order of the Grosses Verdienstkreuz by the German state, and in 1991 he received the French title of Chevalier de l'Ordre des Arts et des Lettres.

The 2014 auction of a Rembrandt print symbolically sums up Kornfeld's success in the international art trade. Lot 6 was *Jan Six*, 1647 (Bartsch/Rovinski/Seidlitz 285), a great print in the finest quality that Kornfeld had in fact auctioned once before, as part of the Weisbach collection in 1954, for the then sensational sum of 34,500 Swiss francs. Exactly sixty years later the family of the buyer had now entrusted it to the care of the same auctioneer. Continuity is Kornfeld's recipe for success. (In 2006, he donated his substantial Rembrandt collection to his hometown of Basel).

In the preface to the catalogue for the company's sesquicentennial (auction 261, 2014), Kornfeld described his position in these terms: 'In future we will still maintain a wide range of international relationships

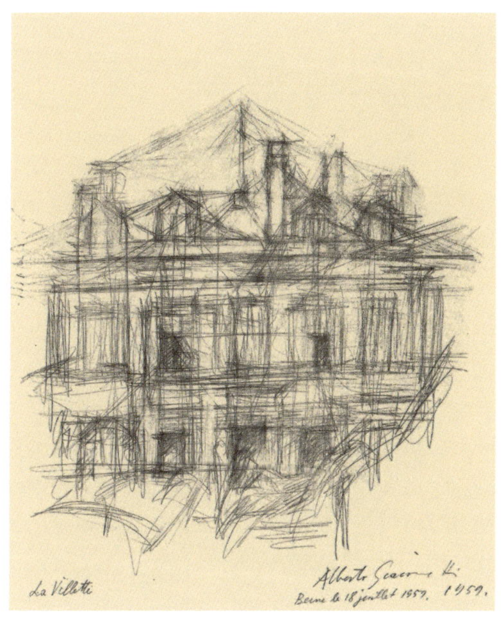

Alberto Giacometti, *The Auction House 'La Villette'*, 1959,
drawing

from our national and regional perspective, placing less emphasis on
sensational turnover figures and more on a quality-oriented intermediary role between seller and buyer. Both should place trust in our
knowledge and our abilities, which have been the basis of our past successes, and which have led to a number of very high prices over the
years.'

Kornfeld's is a traditional firm, based on the eternal components of
all auction houses and galleries: art works, sellers, buyers. Stability and
success are determined by the material, which binds them together!

## 8   London 1957–58 and 1977

The 1957 Sotheby's sale of the William Weinberg collection in London changed the art market.[131] For the first time, an auction was promoted professionally as an event. The Queen herself was invited and attended the preview, attracting great media attention.[132] One year later, when the same firm offered eleven Impressionist paintings from the Goldschmidt collection in the first evening auction ever to be held in Europe, the dress code for the public was (unheard-of) black tie, and bidders could leaf through the first auction catalogue ever to be printed in colour.[133] These two auctions marked the beginning of a new era; henceforth professional marketing created an ambience of expertise and prestige, which pervaded the art works on offer, the auction house and subsequently the entire industry.[134] The Goldschmidt sale went on record as the most expensive art auction of all times, as the Hamilton Palace sale had done over seventy years earlier.[135] It set the tone for the collecting fashion of the years to come. Just as Renaissance art had been collected enthusiastically in the nineteenth century, so the post-war period focused on bright, sun-drenched and paradisiacal Impressionist pictures.

Peter Wilson, who was Sotheby's Chairman from 1958, had not only foreseen this development and done his utmost to facilitate it. He appears to have been one of the first guarantors, as he privately guaranteed a minimum price to a vendor. Half a century later the practice was to become a key acquisition tool.[136] To establish new collecting categories as well as attract a new clientele, he had developed an innovative format with the Mentmore auction in 1977. The dispersal of an aristocratic household in situ meant that provenance became for the first time a visible and sensory experience, even increasing the marketability of lower-value objects. The Country House fashion at the time ensured that a noble house sale would attract not just traditional auction buyers but also those who were interested in particular aspects of the provenance.[137] The Mentmore sale with its white marquees on the bowling green against the backdrop of the castle became the model for similar house sales of the coming decades.

The culmination to date for this development was the castle auction in Baden-Baden almost twenty years later, where Sotheby's was able to sell art and furnishings amounting to 77.58 million deutschmarks.[138] Altogehther, according to UN calculations (UN Comtrade Database), the global import revenue for art and antiquities increased from $220 million in 1962 (the first year of the survey) to $1.74 billion in 1977. Individual transactions were far from carrying price tags in the millions, however. In 1962 Gerald Reitlinger, chronicler of the economic development of the art markets, considered it likely that a picture might sell for one million pounds in the near future but felt that two million would be purely theoretical.[139] Christian Herchenröder estimated that during the second half of the 1970s the entire market, including both primary and secondary markets, made an annual turnover of three billion deutschmarks.[140]

## 8   Peter C. Wilson

When Peter C. Wilson, smartly dressed in his dinner jacket and black bow tie, stepped into the rostrum at Sotheby's in London on 15 October 1958, he began the realisation of his dream to offer works of art at auction to a wider public. Although evening sales were held quite regularly in New York at Parke-Bernet Galleries, such a glamorous event was virtually unknown in austere, post-war Britain. The majority of sales were held during the day and were dominated by dealers for whom auctions provided a significant source of inventory. In only a few areas did private collectors intrude – and then usually in the company of trusted dealers or advisers. It was a very exclusive club.

Peter C. Wilson – or PCW as he was commonly known – brought glamour and the commanding advantage of aristocracy to the arcane business-like proceedings of the auction room. During the ten or fifteen years after the end of the war in Europe, Paris remained the centre of the art world for Impressionist painting and early twentieth-century art. The auction galleries in London were mainly focused on the great Old Masters, the supply of which was already beginning to dry up.

PCW grasped that Impressionist paintings with their bright colours, easy subject matter and abundant supply would be the future of the art market. Furthermore, most of, the great Old Master collections were still in British country houses whose owners were much better connected to the more aristocratic management at Christie's.

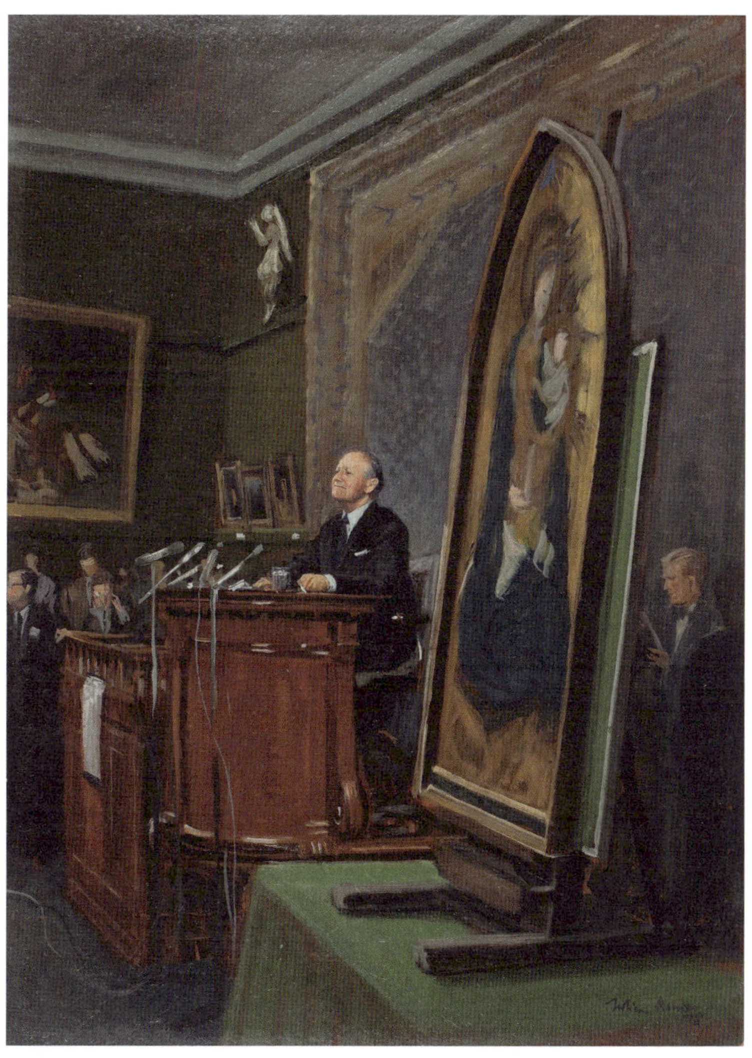

Julian Barrow, *Peter Wilson Conducting the von Hirsch Auction*, 1978,
oil on wood, 36 × 26 cm

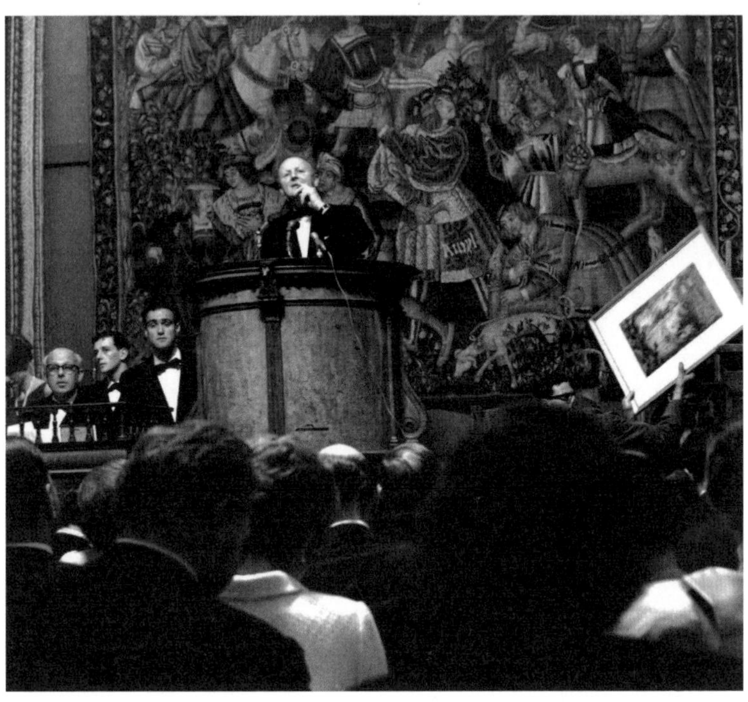

Peter Wilson on the rostrum during the auction to benefit the Institute of Contemporary Arts, London, 23 June 1966, with Walter Feilchenfeldt as Bid Spotter. Feilchenfeldt worked from 1965 in the department of Impressionist and Modern Art at Sotheby's, Paul Cassirer–Walter Feilchenfeldt Archive, Zurich

When I began at Sotheby's in 1961, the department of Impressionist paintings had just been created. The head of the department was Bruce Chatwin, closely followed by Michel Strauss, who arrived a little later. We were all young, and PCW took a great interest in us and in the future of this market. He had a fearless ability to delegate authority to very young people. We were all beneficiaries of his extraordinary foresight in this regard.

Although I do not think he cared at all for very modern art (his personal taste stopped, I suspect, at Picasso) he was very encouraging towards those people at Sotheby's who wanted to drive the auctions into the twentieth century. He enthusiastically supported the sale of the Robert and Ethel Scull collection of Abstract Expressionist and Pop Art in 1973, which was a pioneer sale in this field, although I think he disliked the contents. PCW saw the great advantages to be had in the wonderful world of publicity. All the British newspapers of that time published daily reports of saleroom activity but these were very dry lists of prices achieved and of little interest to the general public. Peter saw the publicity value of a good story – rare objects, sold for huge amounts of money, glamourous gatherings of the rich and famous, fabulous discoveries – these all made good popular copy. The press enthusiastically reported the highlights and the scandals of the auction world (as they continue to do today), and PCW attempted (not always successfully) to manipulate this to Sotheby's advantage.

As an auctioneer, the press routinely described him as 'urbane', 'charming' and 'dignified', and indeed his technique was very polished and unflashy. He spoke quite softly without letting excitement force his voice: his stated intention was to slide the bidding up gently so that the bidders did not fully appreciate the enormous amounts of money that their bid represented – quite the opposite of the current style for dramatic bidding duels. Underneath the urbane and charming façade, however, PCW could be quite ruthless on the rostrum. Every collector has a few stories about how he came to own a particular work of art. If there was one single story that I've heard repeated by many collectors it was the one where the buyer had no intention of going so high but felt hypnotised by Peter Wilson's steely stare when the bid was against him. In fear of being ashamed in the eyes of the great man, the collector would go one bid higher, and then one more! However, when Sotheby's acquired Parke-Bernet Galleries in 1964, this soft but deadly technique did not do so well across the Atlantic. A much more robust style of auctioneering was traditionally appreciated by American audiences.

In the two decades that followed the Goldschmidt sale it became clear to PCW that American collectors, dealers and museums were playing an increasingly important role in many areas of the art market. America was where the money was, and PCW was determined that Sotheby's should be a big presence in this market. When the majority owner of Parke-Bernet Galleries, Leslie Hyam, died in 1962, PCW made a vigorous and successful effort to acquire the company despite relatively little support or enthusiasm from many of his partners in London. In 1965 the takeover was completed, and Sotheby's began the long and sometimes painful exercise of integrating the two companies. Although PCW was not gifted with a great talent for management, he saw a huge future in this unwieldy Anglo-American alliance and indeed was proved right when Christie's opened a saleroom in New York twelve years later.

If PCW did not have the talent of management, it was certainly compensated by his extraordinary 'eye'. His depth and range of knowledge (principally for European art) was very impressive. Endlessly curious about works of art and understanding so clearly the thrill of possession and the excitement of the chase, he was a wonderfully inspiring figure, ideally crafted to lead Sotheby's through three decades of international growth.

I find it amusing (one of PCW's favourite words) to reflect on the present state of the art market and whether he would recognise it as it is today. Certainly he would have no difficulty in understanding the

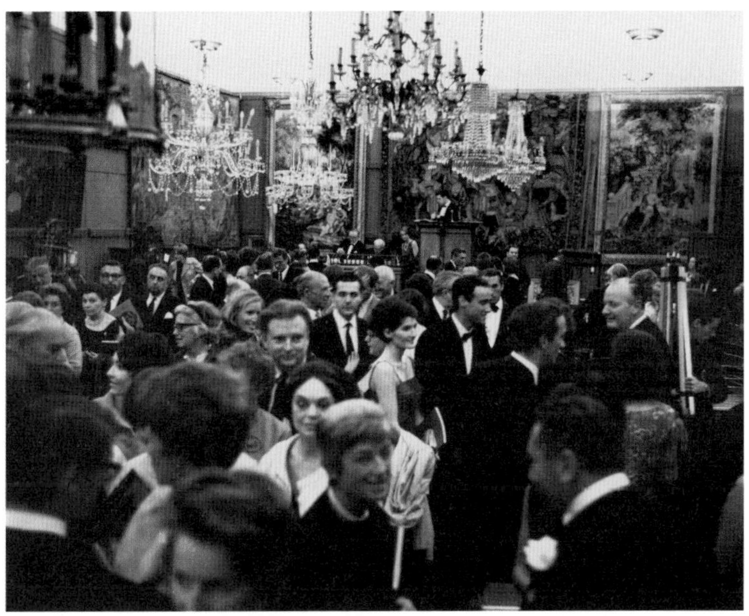

Peter Wilson with Maria and Walter Feilchenfeldt after the ICA auction,
Paul Cassirer–Walter Feilchenfeldt Archive, Zurich

fact that several paintings have been sold for over one hundred million
dollars each. He always believed that great paintings were inexpensive
relative to other things of the same value. 'You can always build a bigger
boat, but you can never make another Cézanne.' However I think he
would be baffled by the way that connoisseurship has given way to
speculation and how art has become so close to a commodity.

## 9   Basel 1964

The London auction houses were comparatively late in discovering the potential of regions across the English Channel and the Atlantic, and in establishing a competitive presence in these markets. The first offices in continental Europe opened in the 1950s.[141] At that time, the assumption was that a potential buyer would find his way independently to any interesting work of art offered in London, and the expansion of a European network was mainly thought to improve access to vendors. Representative offices in New York soon began to look after American buyers and accelerated the development of this market. In 1965 Sotheby's takeover of the leading American auction house Parke-Bernet allowed the firm to hold sales locally; Christie's followed only in 1977 with the opening of auction rooms in Manhattan.[142] A worldwide network of auction rooms and offices came to be established in less than twenty years, enabling the firms to respond as swiftly as any other commercial enterprise to changes in the art market and national collecting trends. They became a model for smaller companies who subsequently also founded offices, employed representatives, or were sometimes even represented by dealers.

A representative office in general does not just process regional valuations, consignments or purchases. The representative employee allows the firm to signal its presence on the regional art scene, and this serves to foster a rewarding exchange with local opinion leaders and to recognise and assess collecting trends. There is a range of options, from a part-time representative who advises clients outside his main professional occupation and can accept smaller consignments, to full office facilities where specialists can receive clients and where the entire administration of potential consignments is coordinated. In addition, there are offices that serve as a venue for regional auctions, while also accepting consignments for other salerooms. If a work of art has to be shipped to the saleroom, transport expenses create a value threshold for the representative. Independently of its quality, an object may or may not therefore be suitable for an auction abroad.

The chronology of office openings mirrors overall economic conditions. The main focus of expansion for both international auction houses was Switzerland, with its great collecting tradition, its affluent collectors, density of collections and ample supply of foreign capital. It seems highly probable that even in the 1960s Swiss clients accounted for the lion's share of European business. Consequently, Christie's opened an office in Geneva in 1968, and Sotheby's in Zurich in 1969. As no competitor was willing to give up the other city to its rival, offices were duly set up in both cities, respectively, and the opening of a Christie's office in Zurich in 1978 completed the quartet. Over many years both firms also maintained a presence in Lugano, and Sotheby's even had an office in Basel. Local auctions followed quickly, since Switzerland was an ideal marketplace for jewellery due to its VAT rate, which in the European context was comparatively low. The two main firms were briefly joined by Phillips in holding sales, be it jewellery, watches and wine offered in a luxury hotel in Geneva, Swiss art in the Zurich Kunsthaus or in the auction house's own rooms in the former department store Ober. The Zurich firm of Koller also opened in Geneva, holding sales there with a distinct profile.[143]

## 9   Anke Adler-Slottke
## Stamps and the First Woman Auctioneer

It is 16 April 1964, and a 22-year-old brunette from Germany stands on the rostrum in the Stadt-Casino Basel with the gavel in her hand. Focused and eloquent, she rapidly switches between German, French, English and Italian while announcing upcoming lots to be auctioned. The lots – small rectangles, with an adhesive backing and scalloped edges – are among the most valuable items available on the stamp collecting market at the time. Her audience of serious-looking and mostly elderly men in suits and ties is attending a sensational event: a part sale of the stamp collection formed by tobacco magnate Maurice Burrus, organised by the renowned stamp auctioneering firm Robson Lowe Ltd from London. Robson Lowe himself is sitting right next to the young woman who assists him. He is three times her age and a veritable beacon of British philately. His firm, which he founded in 1926, is based at no. 50 Pall Mall, London SW1: the leading collectors stamp business in the United Kingdom. Now he wants to expand across the Channel, which is why he has brought his team to Switzerland on this spring day.

This is the first auction by an Anglo-Saxon firm in Switzerland, and the sale of the Burrus's legendary stamp collection on behalf of the Liechtenstein-based Amhelca Trust marks a spectacular start. After the death of the multi-millionaire collector in Lausanne in 1959, the collection had been kept in a Swiss bank vault and is now valued at 35 to 40 million German marks. This is a philatelic dream fulfilled.

The second small sensation of this spring day is the auctioneer: for the first time ever in Switzerland, a woman is taking a sale. On top of everything, she is selling stamps – one of the most male-dominated collecting areas of all – and doing so in a country that did not fully grant women's suffrage until 1971. The heart rates of the assembled connoisseurs accelerate slightly as the 'Double Geneva' and the 'Basel Dove' come up. If the gentlemen in the room are at all surprised about the young woman taking the reins, they nevertheless maintain an impassive façade. The audience is almost entirely male.

Exactly fifty years later the auctioneer recalls the sale from her home in London in the leafy neighbourhood of Swiss Cottage. In the meantime, she has auctioneered in Tel Aviv, Zurich and the German Gera; she has curated exhibitions in Dubai, Moscow, Beijing and Shanghai; she has conceived and co-organised the high-profile Mauerbach auction in Vienna, the first sale since the immediate post-war period of restituted works of art looted during the Second World War. But first times are especially memorable.

Chance, entrepreneurship and pioneer spirit had all contributed to putting the youngest and most novice member of the team in charge of Robson Lowe's first Swiss sale. In 1963, Anke Slottke had rung the bell at no. 50 Pall Mall to enter the offices of the esteemed stamp specialist Robson Lowe. Mr Lowe was a widely respected dealer and auctioneer as well as a gifted historian of philately, whose six-volume *Encyclopaedia of British Empire Postage Stamps* had become an essential reference work. The equally energetic young woman from Hamburg had moved to London four years previously, at the age of seventeen, to complete her education abroad. Her first job was as a temporary typist

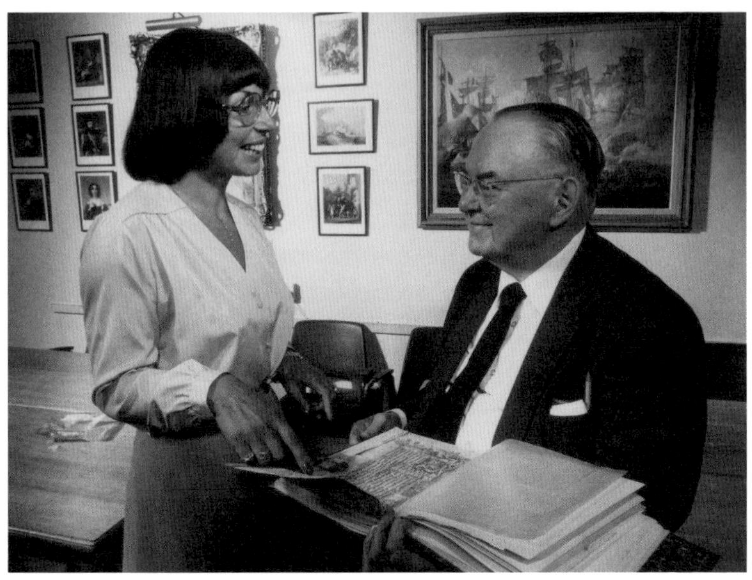

Anke Slottke and Robson Lowe, late 1960s

at a British address as famous as that of Buckingham Palace: 10 Downing Street. An agency then referred her to Robson Lowe Ltd as an assistant. Slottke was keen, multi-lingual, and a useful cataloguer and translator from English and French into German. Lowe employed her. She soon found herself thrown in at the deep end, when she and her colleagues were assigned the task of working with the head of the firm to catalogue and sell parts of the Burrus collection.

Slottke was new to the stamp world. She quickly began to learn about printing and design as well as the economic, historic and cultural background of stamps, and she became familiar with the ways of the collectors in the field, who tended to be introvert and male. When Robson Lowe was instructed to sell parts of the Burrus collection, she was asked to reconnoitre the continental European market. Lowe and his young employee soon formed a relationship based on mutual trust. Slottke suggested Switzerland as the place to sell the Burrus collection. Why? Or rather, why not?

Switzerland's central proximity to France, Italy, Austria and France, the very countries that had produced the stamps to be sold, was of immediate appeal. Furthermore, the country's official languages were German, French and Italian. Last but not least, many potential clients had Swiss bank accounts.

Lowe sent his junior employee to Switzerland on a reconnaissance trip, where she visited Geneva, Zurich and Basel. There was already an established network in the country of auction houses for fine art, prints and coins, including Gutekunst & Klipstein in Bern (since 1919), Fischer in Lucerne (since 1907), Bollag in Zurich (since 1925), Corinphila for stamps in Zurich (since 1925) and Kornfeld in Bern (since 1951). However, no foreign auctioneer had ventured into this territory, and certainly not with stamps. Slottke made her enquiries at the city council offices, compared tax rates, came across a long-established club of stamp collectors in Basel, persuaded the local mayor to confirm the lowest charges in the country and identified Urs Peter Kaufmann as the most important local stamp dealer and business partner for a joint auction sale. Finally, she delivered a full report on all options to her employer at his office.

This trip soon yielded results not just for Robson Lowe but also for Anke Slottke. The co-operation with the Basel stamp dealer Kaufmann was set up, an auction venue found, sale catalogues printed with 176 pages for Switzerland and 52 pages for Austria, and on the aforementioned date in 1964 Robson Lowe put his German employee on the rostrum, with almost no training. From then on, Robson Lowe Ltd was to hold two sales per year in Switzerland, first in Basel and later also in Zurich and Geneva.

The Burrus sale venture was a small triumph. Not least due to his multilingual employee, the self-made man had made his way across the Channel and into continental Europe. Switzerland was clearly an ideal hub for the international stamp collecting community, not just for geographical and strategic reasons but also in commercial terms. Unlike in Britain, European states allowed commissions to be charged to both vendor and buyer. And so, long before European economic integration, a British auction house came to conduct cross-border business on the continent. Anke Adler-Slottke recalls that 'Zurich in the 1960s was really still quite sleepy, but there were good collectors'. Soon the stamp collections she sold were no longer just from Europe but also from Persia, the Ottoman Empire, Hong Kong and China., The clientele was accordingly international, and Lowe maintained close business contacts with the Swiss, Italian, Dutch and French trade.

More pioneering ventures were to follow the Basel enterprise of 1964. In the late 1960s there was even an auction on board the Queen Mary, with telephone connections to New York, Paris, London, Milan and The Hague. Two auctions took place in Tokyo. In addition, the firm participated in great stamp exhibitions, for example in Washington, Mexico and Bangkok. Anke Slottke was a hard-working and energetic contributor to all of them. Driven by the demand for these small historic paper rectangles, she travelled around the world with her employer and went on to sell stamps in Paris, Rome, and Milan. To some extent, their exploits anticipated the global art market.

In 1980 Robson Lowe Ltd was sold to the venerable auction house of Christie's, with whom they had a long business relationship, and Anke Adler-Slottke joined with it. Under these new auspices, stamp

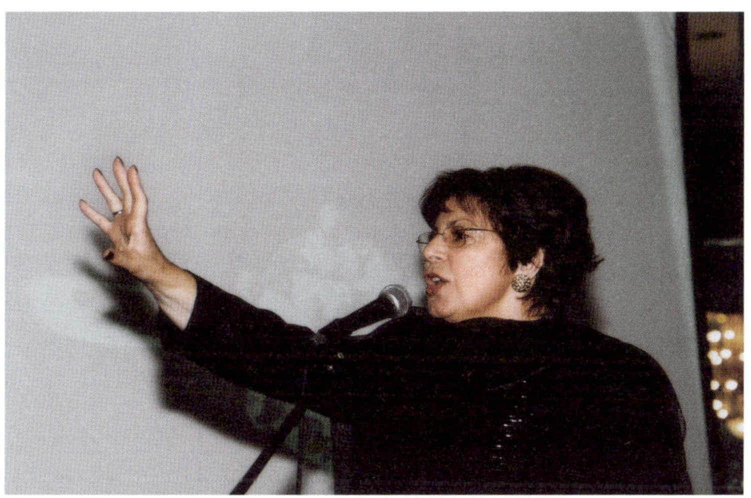

Anke Adler-Slottke at the Mauerbach auction in Vienna, 1996

sales took place in Zurich and Geneva, maintaining the already excellent network.

In the same way that Robson Lowe Ltd had been the vanguard in continental Europe for Anglo-Saxon auction houses, many of which went on to establish branches in Switzerland in the late 1970s, so Anke Adler-Slottke began to pioneer emerging markets for Christie's. From the mid 1990s she became involved in opening up the art market for Impressionist, modern and post-war art in Tel Aviv, Shanghai, Dubai and Moscow. The contacts she established in Israel proved to be invaluable when she led the Mauerbach auction in 1996. To be auctioned were art works confiscated by the Nazis and recovered after the end of the Second World War, works that were considered 'heirless' and had been kept in the custody of the Austrian government until ownership was transferred to the Jewish Community of Vienna.

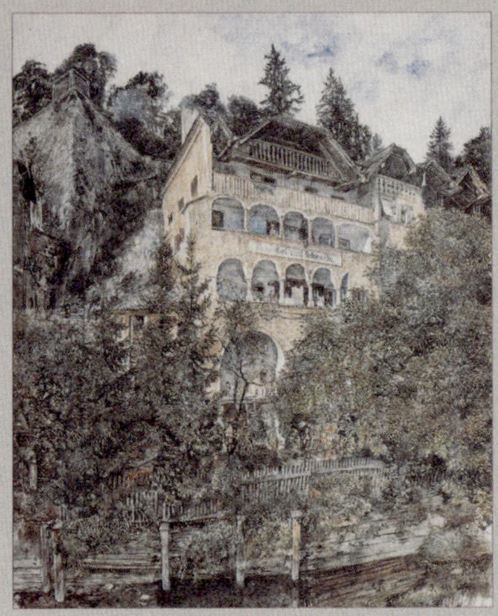


Catalogue of the Mauerbach auction, held in Vienna, 29 and 30 October 1996

Her apprenticeship with Robson Lowe shaped Anke Adler-Slottke's career, since she learned the fundamentals of auctioneering. An auctioneer must be absolutely trustworthy. He or she must ensure that the client has a 'happy experience' but at the same time maintain an educational approach. The auctioneer must establish control while at the same time being somewhat accommodating. She learned the particular acting skills of the auctioneer as well as how to deal with the adrenaline the body pumps out 'massively' during a sale. But the most important lesson she learned from 'Robbie' was that in order to progress, one has to think outside the box.

## 10  New York 1990

In the 1980s the art market experienced the greatest boom of the post-war period. The primary market was pushed to new heights by the increasing demand for contemporary art, which was regarded as a means of achieving social distinction as well as an object of speculation. Sustained investor interest led to a surge in the secondary market. This was encouraged by a change in the wealth tax in the United States, which made donations of art works tax-deductible at a much-reduced rate. This converged with a rising interest by Japanese collectors in Impressionist art, known to have incorporated ideas from the Far East.[144] The decade between 1980 and 1990 saw a price rise of 940 per cent for Impressionist paintings, notwithstanding the stock market crash on 'Black Monday' in 1987. Initially, the anticipated effect on the art market did not materialise, as the sustained price increases had turned art into an alternative investment. In the same year, another world-record price fuelled the market further, as Christie's sold Vincent Van Gogh's *Sunflowers* for £24.75 million. The auction price triggered an avalanche of high-profile auctions of paintings, with world records set in ever more rapid succession. In November 1989 Sotheby's published a list of all auction prices of the month for the first time, which went down in history as 'The Million-Dollar-List'.[145]

The highlight of this soaring development was without doubt the week in May 1990 when the Japanese paper manufacturer Ryoei Saito bought Vincent van Gogh's *Portrait of Dr Gachet* at Christie's in New York for $82.5 million and Auguste Renoir's *Au Moulin de la Galette* at Sotheby's for $78.1 million.[146] This is a perfect example of the boom; it was driven by Impressionist art and often funded by Japanese money. However, shortly before the record sales there were increasing signs that the highest point had passed. A number of individual factors contributed, such as the economic stagnation in Japan, which foreshadowed the Asian crisis of the 1990s, investigations by tax authorities into art purchases, and increasing numbers of unsold lots at big auctions. All prompted speculative investors into withdrawing their funds from the art market. The market for Impressionists collapsed overnight. Many investors lost their bets through panic selling, and art became discredited as an object of long-term speculation. During the final year of the boom, in 1989, the combined turnover of primary and secondary market was estimated at $15 billion.[147] It would take almost a full decade for the art markets to return to the price levels of 1989.

## 10 Starry, Starry Night: *Dr Gachet,* Christopher Burge and Hideto Koyabashi

'We like Japanese painting, we are influenced by it – all Impressionists have that in common', wrote Vincent van Gogh to his brother Theo in June 1888.[148]

Few artists are well known over a century after death. Seldom are their lives well documented. Few have a museum dedicated to them or have been the subject of an award-winning film or a popular song. Rare is the artist who has successfully linked art from two distinct cultures; even rarer the one who has attained the highest prices in the art market. These are some of the unrivalled achievements of the great Dutch artist Vincent van Gogh (1853–1890).

Yet that hard-won reputation was not fully consolidated until May 1990, when Lot 21 of a Christie's auction of eighty-one Impressionist and Modern paintings was sold by Christopher Burge in New York. The record-breaking price of $82.5 million for van Gogh's *Portrait of Dr Gachet* (1890) paid by the Japanese dealer Hideto Koyabashi marked the artist's apogee and, for another fourteen years, the art market's zenith.

Before recalling the historic event of that auction, the contributory factors must be considered. What were the circumstances in which the painting was created? How did the market for this new art evolve?

In 1890 van Gogh wrote to his sister, Wilhelmina, 'What impassions me most – much more that all the rest of my metier – is the portrait, the

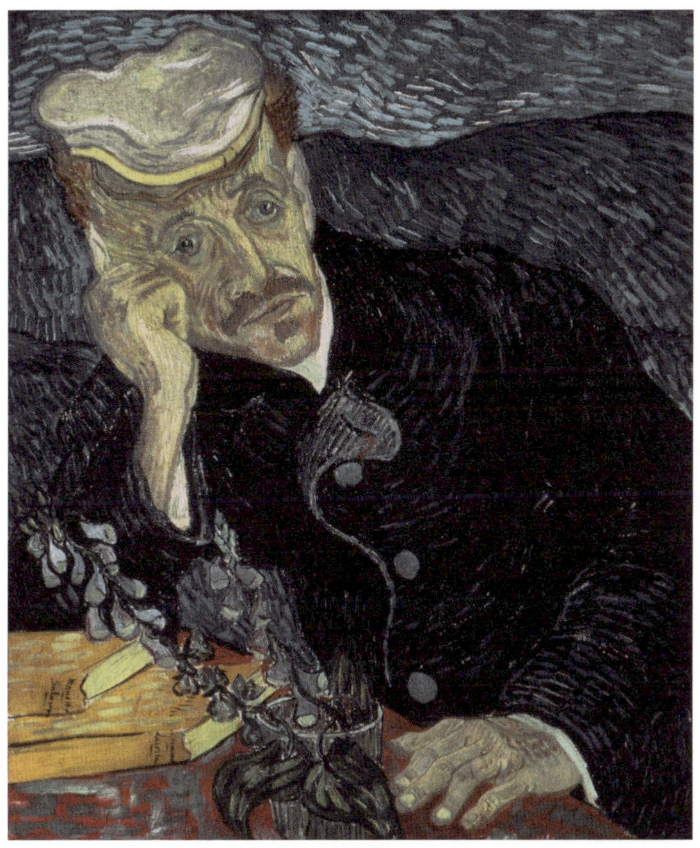

Vincent van Gogh, *Portrait of Dr Gachet*, 1890, oil on canvas, 67 × 56 cm

modern portrait.'[149] He put this passion into practise during the final phase of his short career, while in Provence (1888–90), where he invented Expressionism – or, for *Dr Gachet*, 'an expression of melancholy'.[150] The portrait was one of three images of the sixty-one-year-old psychiatrist, artist and collector with a taste for *Japonisme* (including his only

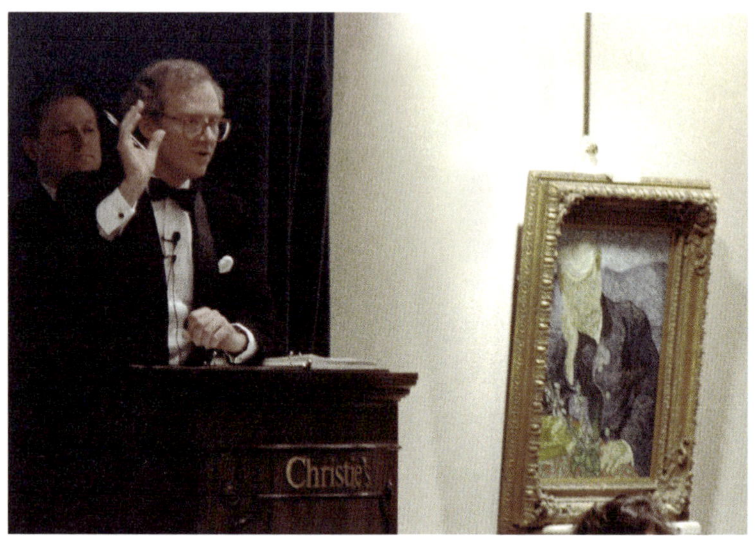

Auction of *Dr Gachet*, Christie's New York, 15 May 1990

known etching) that van Gogh created in May and June 1890. There was also a preparatory sketch.[151]

Characteristics of van Gogh's work, and especially its strong connections to Japanese traditions, appealed to Japanese collectors of Impressionism from the 1920s on, deepening a cultural exchange between Japan and Europe that had begun in the sixteenth century and flourished in the nineteenth.[152] In 1853 the first Japanese objects exhibited in Europe were shown at the Great Industrial Exhibition in Dublin.[153] By the 1890s there was so much Japanese décor 'it became dangerous to walk through a Paris drawing room'.[154]

Encountering Japanese art for the first time, nineteenth-century European painters made use of and drew inspiration from woodblock colour prints, with their sharp contrasts, flat planes, bright colours and compositional arrangements. The immediacy and informality of the Japanese print tradition appealed to painters such as the Impressionists, who were keen to challenge academic values and engage with contemporary life.[155] In the 1860s Edouard Manet and Edgar Degas were the first to make use of devices in prints by such Japanese masters as Katsushika Hokusai and Utagawa Hiroshige.[156]

According to van Gogh's Antwerp correspondence of 1885, he began collecting Japanese prints inspired by the publication *L'art Japonais* and Edmond de Goncourt's novel *Cherie*.[157] Through the dealer Siegfried Bing, van Gogh organised a Japanese print exhibition in 1887 believing that this 'religion' should inspire modern art.[158] Indeed, his first Japanese-inspired paintings in that year were *Agostina Segatori at the Café du Tambourin* and the *Portrait of Julien Tanguy*.[159]

In 1888 he transposed his ideals to Arles with the hope of creating an artistic community that could see 'with a Japanese eye'.[160] His *Self Portrait as Bonze* (Buddhist monk) of 1888 reflects his commitment to the Japanese cause.[161] But before long he lost faith in his abilities to paint in that style, later admitting himself to an asylum in Saint Rémy.

It can be argued that market failure was a cause of van Gogh's illness and short life. After all, artists need patrons and collectors for financial or moral sustenance. We know that Manet earned well from his early years, while van Gogh was subsidised by his art dealer brother, Theo, who worked in a Paris-centred market already selling Impressionists to wealthy American customers from the 1880s.[162] In retrospect, it was observed that, 'in 1900, when van Gogh could have been had for under £50, your grandfather would not have known where to look for one. And in 1913 van Gogh was nearly as dear as Sargent'.[163] Crowning this posthumous achievement, in 1916 van Gogh was the subject of an influential art history book in Japanese translation.[164]

The upturn in van Gogh's auction prices, however, did not arrive until 1921, when *Mademoiselle Ravoux* sold for £4,000. It was re-sold in 1966 for £157,500[165] and again for £7.32 million in 1988. When adjusted for 2013 prices that represents a rise from £154,800 to £2.56 million and £19.36 million. The second chronological benchmark for van Gogh was in 1958 at the legendary Jakob Goldschmidt sale in London. There the *Public Gardens at Arles*, which had been sold for £3,100 in 1928, went for £132,000[166] in a decade when the price of Post-Impressionists shot past the Impressionists.[167] No wonder, Gerald Reitlinger mused in 1970 that 'there must be van Gogh pictures worth a million'.[168]

That came with the Japanese, who had entered the art market in greater force during the 1960s, in their country's decade of 11 per cent annual economic growth.[169] Typically, this new wealth was directed to buying back from abroad their art, which had been exported in quantity since the 1880s.[170] For example, prices for post-seventeenth-century Japanese Netsuke sold at auction typically rose from £200 in 1960 to £1,900–£2,800 in 1969.[171]

By that time Japanese collectors had acquired a taste for buying Impressionist and Modern art at auction. It was a shift enabled by Christie's pioneering the first public auctions at the Tokio Bijutsu Club in May 1969. At the sale Renoir's *Portrait of Madame Henriot* went for £33,875 – only seven years after it had fetched £5,500.[172]

Broader enthusiasm for Impressionism was fuelled by exhibitions that toured Japan in the 1970s, notably of Monet and Degas.[173] Between 1973 and 1987 the Japanese built five hundred museums to house Impressionists and other works.[174] The only restraining factor was the oil price surge in 1973, which caused Japanese collectors to temporarily withdraw from the art market and van Gogh's prices to move little in the 1970s.[175]

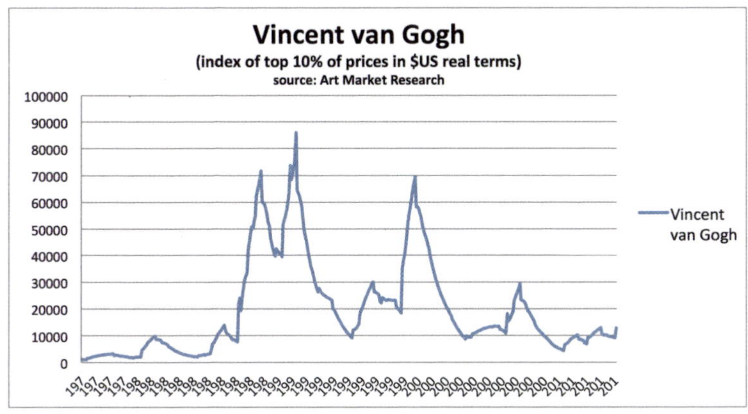


Impressionist and van Gogh price index (Art Market Research)

That changed in April 1985 at the Florence J. Gould sale in New York. Notably, van Gogh's *Landscape with Rising Sun* sold for $9.9 million at Sotheby's – a near world-record.[176] But it was a seismic economic event that catapulted Japanese art buying into the *Dr Gachet* era. In September 1985 the Plaza Accord reversed the US dollar's five-year rise through an agreed international devaluation, resulting in a 51 per cent decline against the Japanese yen by 1987.[177] In effect Japan's international buying power doubled, with dramatic effects in the art market. This was soon reflected in the £22.5 million paid for a version of van Gogh's *Sunflowers* in March 1987 at Christie's by the Japanese company Yasuda Fire and Marine Insurance. In November the *Irises* went for $49 million at Sotheby's – surprisingly just after the October 1987 worldwide stock market crash. Undeterred, the buying continued with an estimated 53 per cent of all worldwide auction sales going to Japan, fuelled by art loans and tax advantages.[178] Confirming Japanese faith in the art market, the gallery owner Yasumichi Morishita bought a 6.4 per cent stake in Christie's.[179]

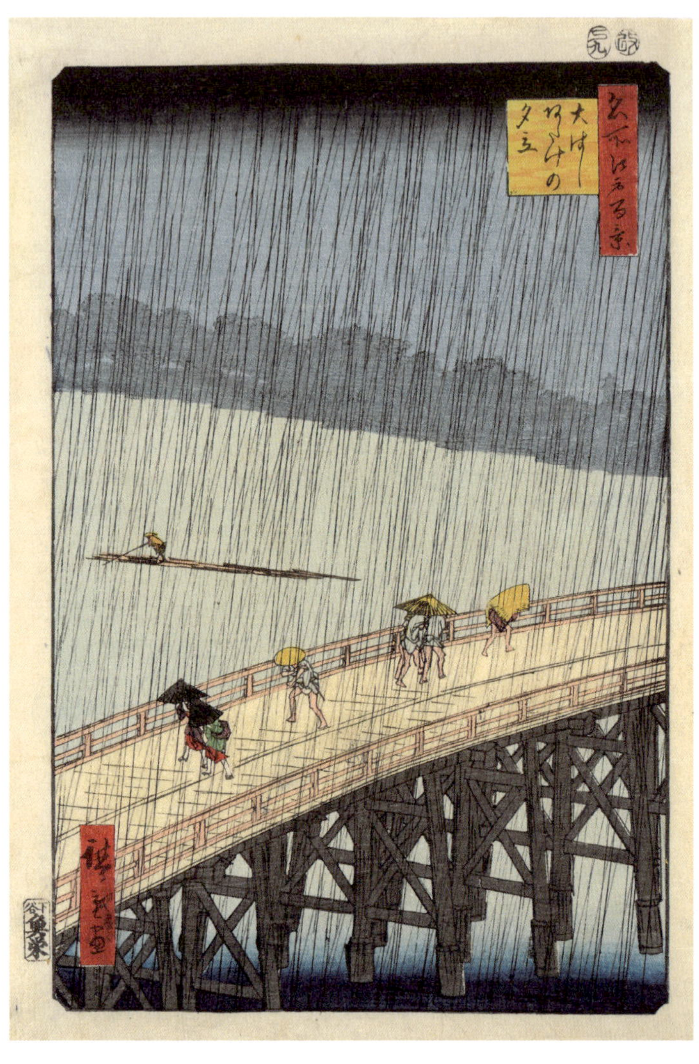

Utagawa Hiroshige, *Sudden Shower on the Great Bridge near Atake*, 1857, woodcut, 37 × 25cm

But there was to be one final push in the art market delivered by van Gogh's *Dr Gachet* on 15 May 1990. Many regarded the portrait as one of the most important works of art for sale, confirmed by the highest estimate ever given until then: $40–50 million.[180]

Siegfried Kramarsky, who bought the painting in 1938, died in 1961. Twelve owners had preceded him, including Theo van Gogh, Ambroise Vollard, and even Hermann Göring.[181] For years the Kramarsky family loaned the painting to the Metropolitan Museum of Art in New York but decided now was the time to sell through Christie's in New York. The family stipulated that the painting must not travel and if the world's stock markets fell more than 25 per cent in a few days, it would be withdrawn – with good reason, because by April 1990 Japan's Nikkei 225 Index had fallen 22 per cent from its January all-time peak of 38,275.[182] Although that did not happen, there were other mitigating factors in the art market.

All was set for a nerve-racking auction in which risk of failure had to be minimised. That included careful distribution of photographs and personal notes to everyone interested, condition reports, attractive payment terms, VIP parties, and primary seating at the auction for a hundred dealers and collectors. By the time of the sale, Christopher Burge had fifty to a hundred bids on his book, aware that prices had been guaranteed up to $50 million. For *Dr Gachet* the price reserve was set at $35 million.[183]

The auction began tentatively. Many of the early lots sold below their estimates, with some unsold. Then came Lot 21 for *Dr Gachet*. The bidding was started at $20 million, rising quickly to the reserve before faltering at $40 million. Then from the back of the room the Japanese dealer, Hideto Koyabashi, raised his arm at $41 million. This was surprising because Koyabashi had never shown interest in the painting at

Christie's. The counter bidder, Maria Reinshagen, on behalf of a Swiss collector, helped push the price up to $50 million. Amid applause and whistles the van Gogh record for the *Irises* was exceeded. But the bidding continued:to $55 million, $60 million, $65 million and $70 million. From there Reinshagen bid more slowly to $74 million. Koyabashi came back with $75 million. Privately his last bid. Burge's gavel fell. The lot sale had lasted only three minutes. Including commissions the final price paid was $82.5 million (£44.1 million).[184]

In an auction that ended with 24 of 81 lots unsold – or 42 per cent of the estimated auction value – the *Dr Gachet* sale was even more significant. The high point of the Impressionist and Modern art market was 1989, when less than 15 per cent of lots sold below estimate. Christie's chairman, Lord Carrington, observed that the total sum paid for *Dr Gachet* was the same as the company's combined annual sales fifteen years earlier.[185] But it had to end. As *The Economist* observed in December 1990, 'when it can cost more to buy a painting than to set up a medium-sized business, a market correction looms.'[186]

But the market for van Gogh was not subdued for long. In 1998, his *Portrait de L'artiste Sans Barbe* (1889) sold at Christie's for $71.5 million, becoming the seventeenth most expensive painting ever sold at auction – not far behind *Dr Gachet* at tenth.[187]

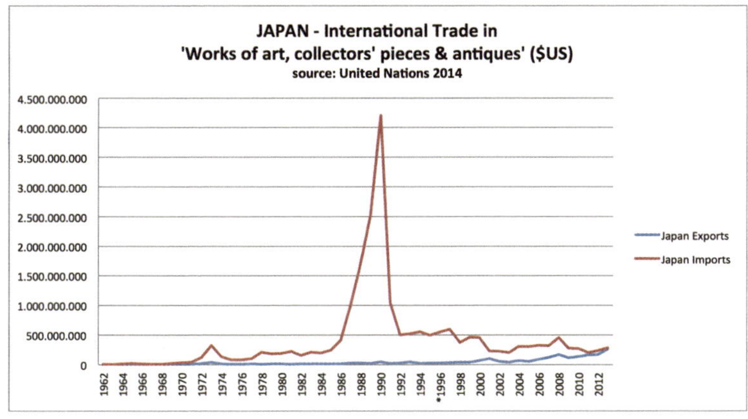


Graph detailing works of art and other art objects imported into and exported from Japan from 1962 to 2012

## 11  New York, London, Geneva and Zurich 2000–01

The decade of the 1990s ended with two sensations: in 1999, Sotheby's announced a surprising foray into the Internet business, and Christopher Davidge, Christie's CEO at the time, admitted to price-fixing. He declared that he had been in collusion with Sotheby's, his company's main competitor, about prices for services. As both firms held a joint market share of circa 90 per cent, this admission was relevant under antitrust legislation in the US. It was found by a US federal court that Davidge and his counterpart at Sotheby's, Diana D. Brooks, had agreed on the seller's commission from 1992 as well as on the buyer's premium from 1995. The court sentenced both companies to pay damages in the millions, and the companies' respective CEOs and chairmen resigned.[188]

The loss of trust by the clients in the integrity of both houses opened the field to a new and influential competitor. Bernard Arnault – CEO of LVMH (Louis Vuitton Moet Hennessy) and, as such, a competitor of Francois Pinault, who owned Christie's as part of the luxury conglomerate PPR (Pinault Printemps Redoute, today Kering) – bought the Phillips auction house with the aim of transforming it into a competitor at the top end of the market. LVMH millions funded a relaunch, including a new corporate identity and an expanded team of experts. Arnault secured the support of the art dealers and former Sotheby's directors Simon de Pury and Daniella Luxembourg. As early as November 2000, de Pury was the auctioneer for the rebranded Phillips first New York sale. The art dealership and the auction house were merged into Phillips, de Pury & Luxembourg, while the Zurich gallery of De Pury & Luxembourg continued parallel operation in the primary market.[189] In 2001 it was decided to focus the core business on a few significant collecting areas and to hand over smaller departments to Bonhams. Investments did not stop at the presentation of the company and new staff. Deep pockets allowed the auction house to guarantee minimum prices to potential sellers.[190] As a result, works from the collection of the famous art dealer Heinz Berggruen were consigned, attracting extensive media interest.

The competition did not suffer as much as expected, however. While the number of important consignments at Christie's and Sotheby's did see some reduction, the business network continued to function. With new – and untainted – CEOs at their helms, scandal was soon forgotten.[191] To the disappointment of its parent company, Phillips found it increasingly hard to gain a foothold in the market. When LVMH share prices fell in 2002, Arnault decided to withdraw from the firm and sold it to de Pury and Luxembourg. It went on to become Phillips, de Pury & Company in March 2004, when Luxembourg departed. One of the 'companies', the Russian Mercury group, successively bought de Pury's shares. When he left in 2013, the name of the company reverted simply to Phillips.[192]

In the end, the vision of challenging the two major houses and joining their ranks as eye-level competitors proved impossible to realise. Nevertheless, the process was an important development; concentrating on a few collecting areas brought about the creation of a boutique auction house. Phillips became a stylish role model for many imitators in the world's capitals as well as on the Internet. The combination of different firms, originally the result of a merger, which had been regarded as a risky mix, was to become the pioneer of a new kind of art dealership, combining auctions, private sales and art advising.

## 11   The Dream of a Boutique Auction House Phillips, de Pury & Luxembourg

By the end of 1996, Simon de Pury and I decided to leave Sotheby's in order to create De Pury & Luxembourg Geneva. By then, I was already on my twenty-sixth year of work in art world institutions in Jerusalem, Tel-Aviv and, later, Vienna. Within those twenty-six years, there were thirteen years at Sotheby's in Israel and Switzerland, and I had the feeling I should try to work independently. We were both experienced and well motivated.

So in 1997 we opened our offices and viewing rooms at no. 29 Quai des Bergues in Geneva. We specialised in private sales and exhibitions of Impressionist, Modern and Contemporary Art. We assembled around us a group of collectors, curators, estate lawyers and accountants whom we advised and with whom we searched for the highest quality of works of art to be found. During our few years of work we sold several dozen works to American and European museums and foundations, created a Contemporary Art fund (Pisces), valued some of the largest collections and artists' estates and opened a large gallery in Zurich.

We had a small but excellent infrastructure: one office, one gallery, one space in the free port, and three great experts: Andrea Caratsch, David Breuer-Weill and Olivier Berggruen. Helmut Newton photographed us for our initial business announcement, and other artists such as Tina Barney, Malick Sidibé and Robert Wilson followed, by

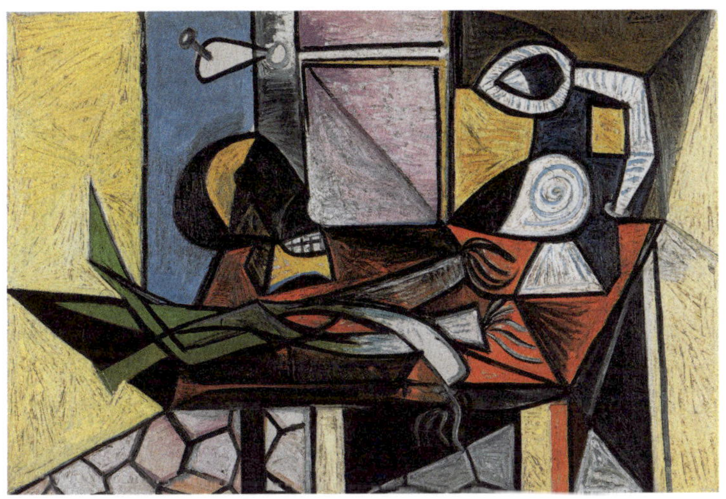

Pablo Picasso, *Poireaux, crâne et pichet*, 1945, oil on canvas, 80 × 130 cm, formerly in the collection of Nathan and Marion Smooke

creating the annual De Pury & Luxembourg cards for the new year. In our company's fourth year (2000), Bernard Arnault – head of the luxury conglomerate LVMH – was actively looking to enter into the auction business. He started pursuing an acquisition of Phillips, and later of Bonhams in England and Tajan in France. The aim was to turn Phillips into a high-end auction house and keep Bonhams as it was. Both Phillips and Bonhams targeted predominantly the middle-market. Both houses were running more than a hundred sales per year, and were quintessentially British brands.

But Arnault wanted a market for his new auction house that was entirely different from the one Phillips and Bonhams had targeted in the past. He was looking to take one house and turn it into a new entity that would ultimately manage to break the Sotheby's/Christie's duopo-

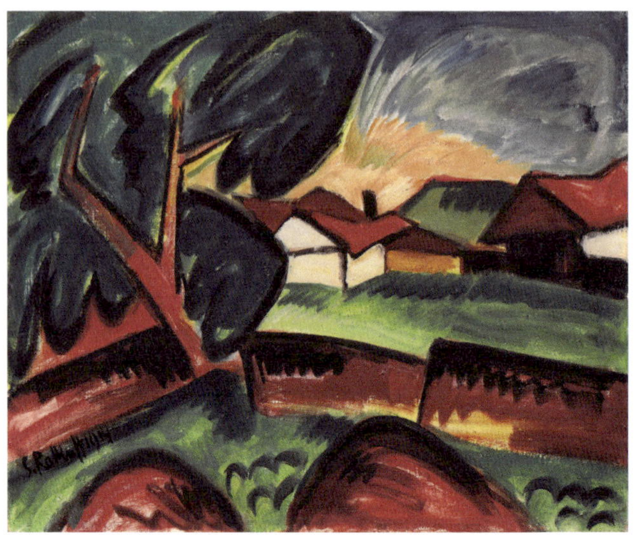

Karl Schmidt-Rottluff, *Gehöft* (The grange), 1914, oil on canvas, 78 × 91 cm, formerly in the Smooke collection

ly. At the time, the market was still very much in the thralls of the class action suit against these top auction houses. And while the atmosphere around them was tense and pessimistic, it set the stage for other players to reassess – and in the case of Arnault, to ultimately challenge – their strong hold over the art market.

The negotiations between our company and LVMH went on for six months, and Phillips, de Pury & Luxembourg came to be. Phillips was founded in 1796, and Bonhams three years prior. Turning a new leaf in a small business whose foundations have existed for centuries is an enormous undertaking. And the art world, being a traditional milieu, is quite skeptical to newcomers.

We focused our main efforts on building a new designated auction venue in New York and moved to a beautiful building at 3 West 57th Street,
which had been renovated with the help of LVMH's tastemaker Katel
Le Bourhis. In London we moved from the old Phillips building at no.
101 New Bond Street to Grosvenor Street, and in Geneva our old De Pury
& Luxembourg offices on the Quai des Bergues were turned into auction
offices. We also kept an office and saleroom in Zurich alongside maintaining our activities in the newly-appointed contemporary gallery of
De Pury & Luxembourg at Kreuzstrasse 54.

Alongside these new spaces we had to source the great collections
that would justify our ambitions undertaking. The magic appeared in
the figure of Heinz Berggruen, one of the best collectors and dealers of
the second half of the twentieth century. He had just decided to gift the
city of Berlin his core Modernist collection and to sell those works that
did not fit with the rest. And so, we were fortunate enough to secure for
our first major sale seven Cézannes and three Van Goghs, among others.
The sale took place on 7 May 2001, achieving the record price for a work
of art at the time: $38,500,000 for Paul Cézanne's *La Montagne Sainte-Vic-
toire* of 1888–90.

In the November season of the same year we sold the collection of
major California-based collectors Nathan and Marion Smooke, with sev-
enty-two major late nineteenth-century and early twentieth-century
paintings by Edgar Degas, Fernand Léger, Constantin Brancusi, Henri
Matisse and Amedeo Modigliani, among others. The sale total was
$86,193,700 with more than 93 per cent of lots sold, and seven artist re-
cords were set. On the same day we sold the wonderful collection of forty-nine works from the estate of Diethelm Hoener. The group included
several fine examples of German Expressionism as well as a distinguished
group of works by Emil Nolde. Forty-six of the forty-nine works sold.

In the first two years of Phillips, de Pury & Luxembourg, we sold over five hundred million dollars worth of art. The guarantees we gave for the great collections were not always covered, but it was the only option we had when entering into that high-end market. It was also not a strategy we wanted to apply as a long-term vision. These sales brought to us many more collectors than we could have dreamed of, and we were able to compete alongside Sotheby's and Christie's on estates and collections such as Arturo Schwarz's collection of Marcel Duchamp's readymades. Schwarz was the scholar who compiled the Duchamp catalogue raisonné and was in charge of the production of the readymades from 1964. The auction took place on 13 May 2002 and included fourteen iconic readymades. The highlight of the sale was *Bicycle Wheel* of 1913, which sold for $1,700,000 (a record price for Duchamp at the time). The sale of that collection, and the significant catalogue that we published for it, were a high point of my time in the auction business.

We regarded each catalogue as an entity with a logic all its own, and adapted the format and design concept to it. Our emphasis on design was felt throughout. Katel le Bourhis advised us on several aspects, ranging from the above-mentioned new building in New York to the appearance of the lobby, the auction room and even our offices. There was a buzz of newness and a sense of enormous challenge. The business had to be built from scratch, including client lists, teams of researchers and experts, and the entire administrative operation.

Our selling categories were: Impressionist, Modern, Contemporary, American and Swiss Art, Jewellery, Watches and Wristwatches, European Furniture, Twentieth and Twenty-first Century Design, Art and Photographs, and we conducted auctions in New York, Geneva and Zurich.

We were able to attract a great team of experts such as Aurel Bacs, David Bennett, John D. Block, David Breuer-Weil, Andrea Caratsch,

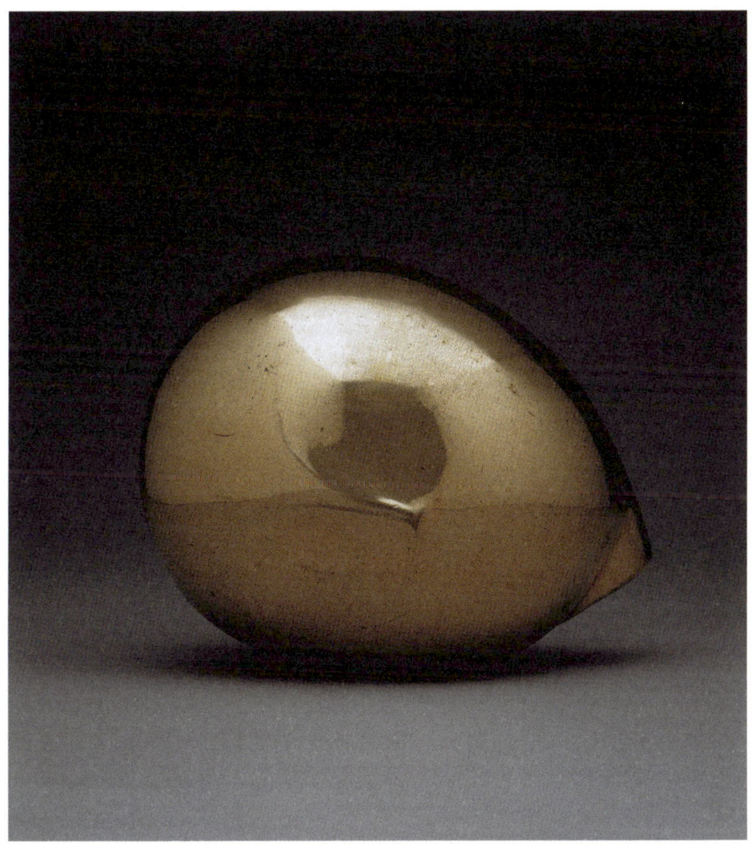

Constantin Brancusi, *Prometheus*, 1911, bronze, height: 13 cm

Angelina Chen, Andrea Crane, Amalia Dayan, Joshua Holdeman, Aileen Hovanessian, Betty Krulik, Lory Kutsher, Michael McGinnis, Thierry Millerand, Dr Michaela Neumeister, Jutta Nixdorf, Alexander Payne, Irene Stoll, Michel Strauss, Prince Dimitri of Yugoslavia and James Zemaitis.

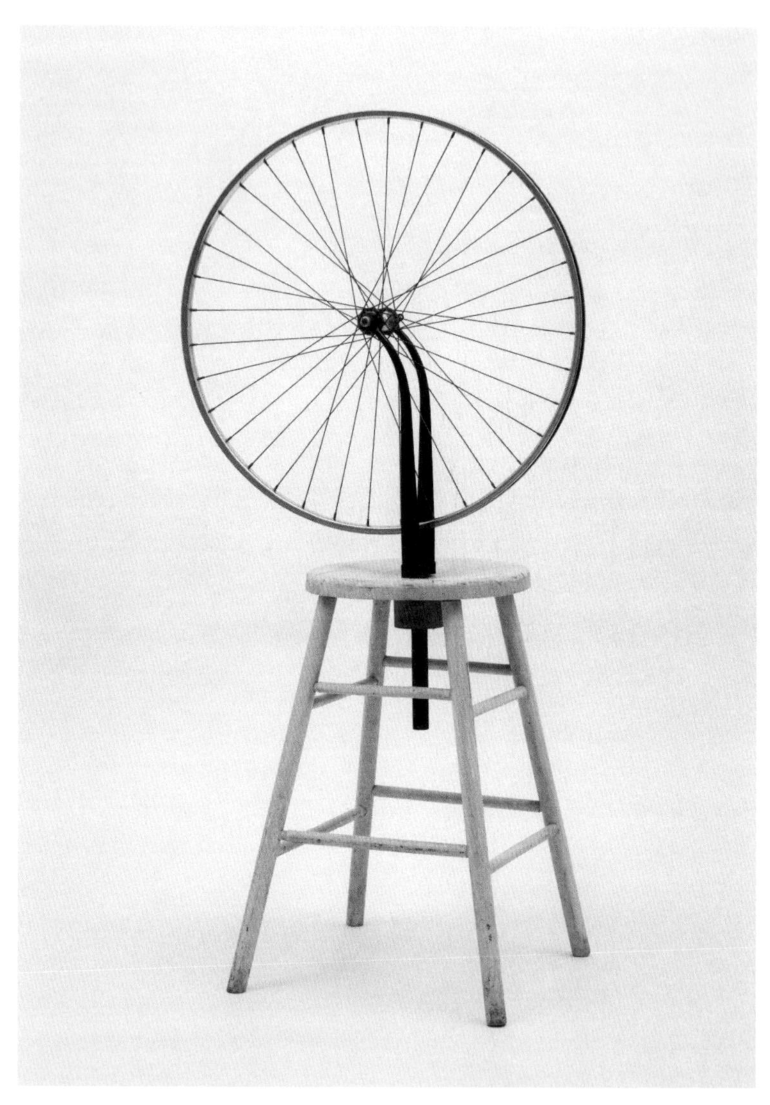

Marcel Duchamp, *Roue de bicyclette*, 1913/1964, readymade, height: 127 cm

After the terrorist attacks on the World Trade Centre, LVMH's stock –
like that of other luxury companies – plummeted, and in 2002 the company decided to reduce their stake in Phillips. Soon after, in 2003, LVMH
sold the remainder of Phillips, de Pury & Luxembourg to Simon and
me; and at the beginning of 2004, I went on to sell my half to Simon and
left the auction world to pursue my initial dream of private sales and
galleries. Since then, the art market has adopted the guarantees, the
beautifully designed auction catalogues, the interior design and the
rest of the packaging of auctions as the norm.

The dream of building a boutique auction house can still be
achieved. Endurance and long-term commitment are essential to the
game, in addition to knowledge of the market's experts and leaders. But
above all, the magic depends on the few key collectors and their truly
great works of art.

## 12   Paris 2001–2009

Paris was not only the birthplace of Modernism but also of its commercial procurement. During the second half of the nineteenth century and at the beginning of the twentieth century, Paris was for decades the centre of the international art trade. The introduction of *Droit de suite* in 1920, the German occupation during the Second World War, and most of all the limitations imposed by the antiquated French auction laws have ended this supremacy.[193]

The regulations for auction sales date back to an edict issued by Henry II in 1552. Only the so-called *commissaires-priseurs*, possessing a state license, were allowed to hold auctions. These licenses were only granted to natural persons, and only provided they were French![194] The only permitted venue of an auction was in the rooms of the Hôtel Drouot, the seat of the association of commissaires-priseurs.[195] International auction houses therefore merely had representatives in France who exported consigned art works abroad. In 1992, the president of Sotheby's France, Laure de Beauvau-Craon, brought the case before the European Court of Justice. It was obvious that the French auction regulations violated European laws, in particular the freedom to provide services as set out in the Treaty of Rome. On 21 July 2001 new auction legislation was passed.[196] Auctions are now no longer conducted by state-appointed sworn officials but by commercial companies.[197] International firms in particular had been eagerly awaiting the opening of the market.

Sotheby's moved its offices and new salerooms to the former Galerie Charpentier across from the Elysée Palace, while Christie's took over a space formerly occupied by Galerie Artcurial on Avenue Montaigne. A former established commissaire-priseur, François de Ricqlès, became president of Christie's France.

All other commissaires-priseurs transformed their enterprises into commercial companies, and despite initial concerns have been able to assert themselves very well against the new international competition. Their contacts, which in some cases have been established over generations, are an important factor. The national pride of the clientele plays a part, too – many French clients shy away from consigning art to 'foreign' companies. It is not surprising that François de Ricqlès – who made the transition from his position as a leading commissaire-priseur before the reform to a senior position at an international firm with its resources and networks – maintains a top position in the competition for desirable collections, estates and art works. He decided after all to join the most 'French' of international houses, as Christie's has been part of François Pinault's luxury conglomerate since 1997.

From the first year after the opening of the market, Christie's became the largest auction house in France. The YSL sale helped to consolidate this position. In 2009, France contributed €2.47 billion (19 per cent) to a global auction market of €12.9 billion. Christie's turnover in France was €440 million, which corresponds to a market share of 18 per cent of in France.[198]

## 12  Meeting Saint Laurent

Yves Saint Laurent came into my life in 1976. Aged sixteen, I got to experience my first YSL haute couture catwalk show at the Hotel Intercontinental on the Rue Castiglione! Gustav Zumsteg, owner and *createur* of Abraham's, one of the most prestigious silk producers in Zurich. had made it possible.

Saint Laurent had worked closely with Abraham's since the early days of his career, and he and Zumsteg had become close personal friends. On the rare occasions when Saint Laurent travelled to Zurich, the two of them always had dinner at the Kronenhalle restaurant, which was owned by Zumsteg's mother Hulda. YSL loved the place. Many years later, when I had become a designer myself and showed my own collections in Paris, I returned once more to the Kronenhalle, where Gustav Zumsteg told me that over many years he had had telephone conversations with Saint Laurent every Sunday afternoon.

At that time my parents used to go to Paris and Rome twice a year to see the haute couture shows in July and January. It would have been impossible for them to obtain another ticket for me, so there was great delight that Zumsteg had done so. To this very day, the catwalk show in July 1976 remains an eye-opening experience for me. It shaped my work in many ways and continues to inspire me. From that moment on I admired Yves Saint Laurent's creations. Each collection had its theme and its dramaturgy; each catwalk show was a harmonious composition

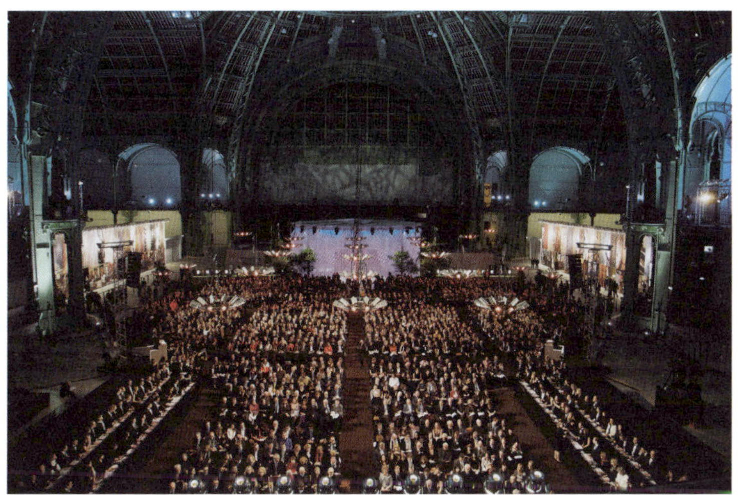

Auction room at the Grand Palais, Paris, 23 February 2009

of astonishing individual statements about the overall picture that defined the season.

During this second half of the 1970s YSL had reached his peak. He designed trailblazing collections such as *Les Ballets Russes* (autumn/winter 1976), *Dolman, Les Romantiques et Les Espagnoles* (spring/summer 1977), *Chinoise et Opium* (fall/winter 1977), *Hommage à Picasso et Diaghilev* (autumn/winter 1979), *Les Courses 'Deauville'* (spring/summer 1980) – each one better than before. He was the best in his profession at this time. *'Le roi de la mode'* declared the fashion newspaper *Women's Wear Daily* on its cover for an edition devoted to his autumn/winter collection. *WWD* is the only newspaper reporting exclusively on fashion, perfume, jewellery, accessories, society and the people who shape the profession in every way. Even as a teenager I was engrossed in reading what happened in the world and far away from my Swiss home town of St Gallen.

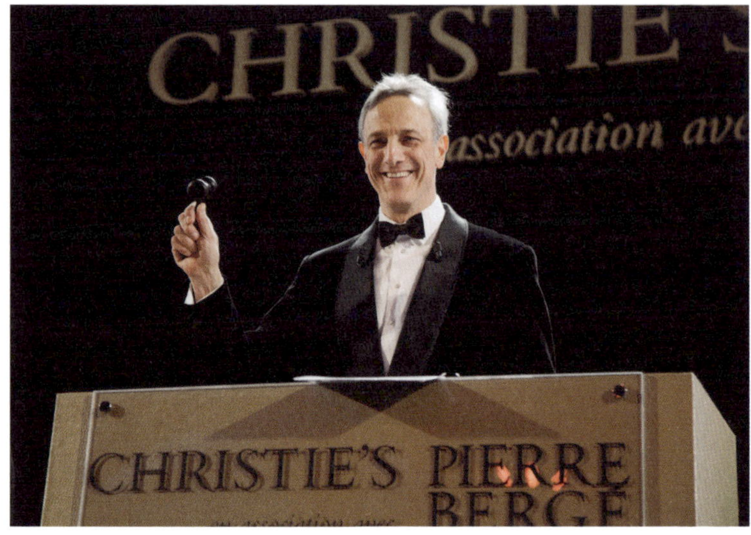

François de Ricqlès at the YSL evening auction

I was to accompany Zumsteg to two more Yves Saint Laurent catwalk shows. The room was always packed with golden Louis XV chairs. The models strode onto the catwalk through a grand portal decked with flowers and paraded the room beneath the huge golden chandeliers. No others left their mark on the fashion of the time like YSL did. The most elegant women wore those incomparable trouser suits and skirt suits with the marvellously sculpted tailored shoulders. There were jackets and blazers, fabulous coats, sporty caban jackets, tailored trouser suits, safari blouses or shirtdresses, jumpsuits even then and more than once, the uncompromising tuxedo and perfect day coat or coat dresses, which gave a just superficial impression of being cut very simply. In addition, there were severe shirts and feminine bow blouses, and his virtuoso cocktail and evening dresses.

His sense of colour was unsurpassed. He was able to combine three or more colours in the most sophisticated way. No other designer or couturier measured up to this talent! Classy women wore YSL, and they could do so from morning till night. His clothes met all requirements of his clientele with unprecedented modern and simultaneously classic style. He met the zeitgeist. Yves Saint Laurent gave women's fashion all those forms of clothing that were new at the time and still remain valid; he formulated the future of timelessness.

Everything that happened with and around Yves Saint Laurent continues to matter to me. I was able to visit his two-story apartment in Rue du Babylone in the seventh arrondissement in Paris just before the contents were removed for auction sale; the apartment was in the condition in which he must have left it when he died on 1 June 2008. At the request of a friend, I was able to see all of this in situ before the collection went on public view at the Grand Palais for three days. Jonathan Rendell – vice president at Christie's New York, who was in charge of the sale – made this private viewing possible. Then, over three unforgettable days in February 2009, the collection was sold and scattered in all directions by the art-loving public.

The rooms of the apartment immediately reminded me of Jean Michel Frank: simple, high oak-panelled walls, windows and rooms that were filled with art – bronzes, pictures, sculptures – as well as with furniture and other objects spanning two thousand years of art history. Together with his partner Pierre Bergé, Yves Saint Laurent had collected all of this with an unfailing eye over fifty years. The ensemble often seemed casual or incidental, giving the impression that the flat was still inhabited and that each object was in the place chosen by Yves Saint Laurent. The French bulldog Moujik and the butler were still there and it seemed to me as if Yves Saint Laurent were still alive.

The drawing room for intimate social events with its fireplace was entirely clad with mirrors. Claude Lalanne needed almost ten years to finish all fifteen mirrors. Branches and leaves flourished from the frames made of gilt bronze and copper, they concealed lighting. On the sills, lamps by Eugen Brandt in the shape of a cobra gave a warm light. There was no daylight in this room.

The main drawing room was dominated by the wood sculpture *Madame L.R.* by Constantin Brancusi standing before a large mirror above the fireplace. Framing the mantlepiece were Paul Cézanne's *Montagne Sainte-Victoire vue des Lauves*, Gericault's Portrait of Alfred and Elisabeth Dédreux, Picasso's *Instruments de musique sur un guéridon*, and Léger's *La tasse de thé*. Many of the pictures in Yves Saint Laurent's collection translated into a visible inspiration for his collections in the late 1970s. His passion for the artists and the pictures he had purchased were transferred to evening dresses or jackets decorated with embroideries or collages.

We were then led through the long oak-panelled corridor towards the rooms with the beautiful Art Deco lamps by Edgar Brandt. Finally we were able to see the lower ground floor at garden level, with its library and the décor by Jacques Grange. Two paintings by Piet Mondrian hung in the library, reminding me immediately of the Mondrian dresses, where they were joined by the much-loved sculptural sheep by the duo François-Xavier and Claude Lalanne. In the same room I also saw the early Warhol portrait of Yves Saint Laurent, and the YSL logo designed by A. M. Cassandre – possibly the best logo ever created in our profession. Viewing the fabulous 'bar for friends' made out of silver nickel-plated brass and marble, with its egg-shaped crystal ice cooler, recalled long nights and receptions in the library or the garden, when Yves Saint Laurent was still well. There were white chairs on the terrace designed

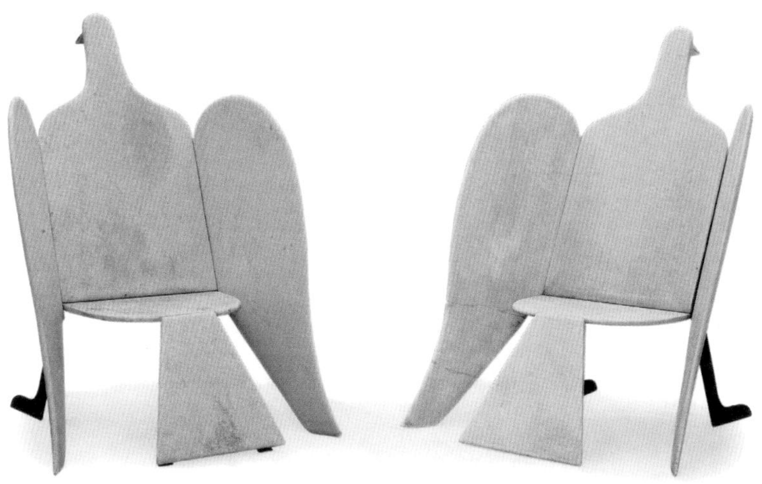

François-Xavier Lalanne, *Oiseaux de Marbre, Grand Modele*, 1974,
marble and steel, 120 × 90 × 105 cm

by Lalanne from white marble and steel. These so-called 'bird chairs'
were evocative of doves by Henri Matisse.

The entire apartment gave a very real and natural impression
throughout the living spaces, yet the standard set by Saint Laurent was
manifest in every single object. There was a dense and rich display of
pictures, sculptures and objects, but nothing appeared contrived or
museum-like, except perhaps the small cabinet lined like a *Wunder-
kammer* in red velvet that Jacques Grange had designed especially for
the objects on the lower ground floor. It contained a collection of cam-
eos together with a large Chinese Buddha from the Ming Dynasty.

In preparation for the auction, this *Gesamtkunstwerk* of a collection
was presented as an apartment at the Grand Palais. It is thought that

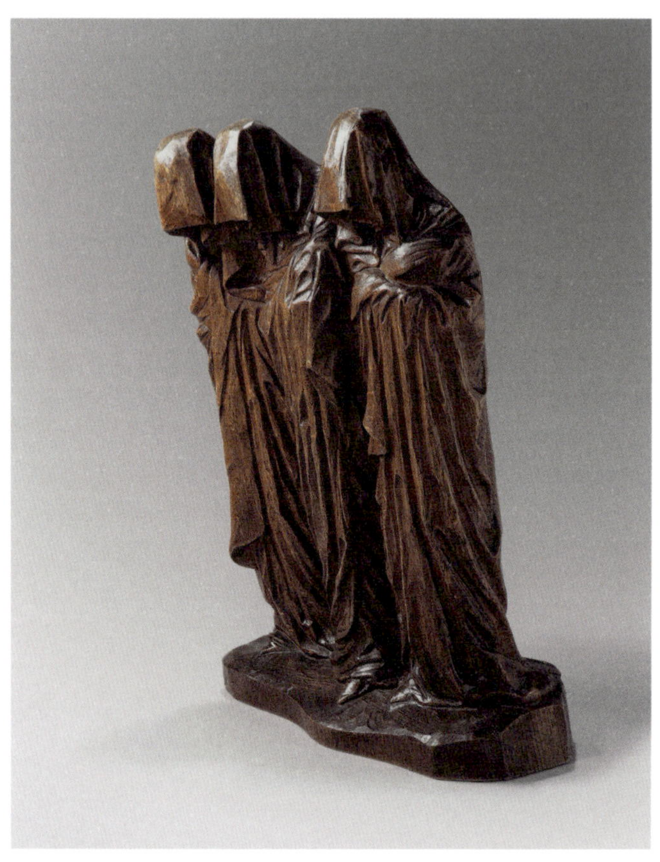

George Minne, *Les Saintes Femmes au Tombeau*, or *Les Trois Pleureuses*, 1896, varnished oak, 61 × 41 × 20 cm

the sale was originally meant to take place in New York, but Pierre Bergé ensured that Christie's auction would become a national, European and ultimately worldwide posthumous celebration of arguably the greatest couturier and fashion designer of all times.

Even when the preview opened, thousands of Parisians, French people and art lovers queued over a hundred meters. It was impressive to see how at Bergé's initiative all of France was celebrating the genius YSL with national pride. No other country is likely to have offered a comparable tribute and similar posthumous fame to a personality from the world of fashion. It was a moving testimony by the city of Paris and the French state to a unique life's work. The preview was not ticketed, and anybody who wanted to see it would thus be admitted. To see so many come and accept the long waiting times seemed to me the last accolade from contemporaries from all walks of life, from the people in general, to the life's work and to the much loved and yet so sad King of Fashion, Yves Saint Laurent.

Everything about Yves Saint Laurent was unparallelled, and so was the auction, which made history as the 'sale of the century'. It was to date the biggest sale of a private collection in both volume and revenue in Europe, with seven hundred and thirty-three objects and over one thousand bidders. It took place in the biggest and most elegant auction room in the world, with thirteen thousand square metres. I still regret today that I hesitated in the face of the overwhelming number of bidders and did not buy anything. Today I cannot forgive myself for not having taken the sculpture by Minne home to St Gallen!

There will never be anybody like him again. For all those who were privileged to meet him, Yves Saint Laurent remains unforgettable and unique in his naturalness and greatness.

## 13 New York 2004

Contemporary Art was the signature style of the millennium. Collecting had turned into a society game even during the previous decades; it has since become part of an elite lifestyle to fill one's private sphere with art.[199] At the same time, the avant-garde characteristics of contemporary art became more predominant, as art was increasingly charged with metaphysical and philosophical content. In order to be avant-garde, it had to challenge more than ever established conventions of taste and perception. This led to a change in status for art ownership: previously, art had been purchased to signal wealth, and in order to imply a tradition of wealth it could not be too new. Now art became not just a status symbol because of its price but also because it allowed one to infer that the owner possessed a level of education and interest to engage with the works. For the first time, art ownership was endowed with the double meaning of other status symbols.[200]

Contemporary art has been sold at auction since the mid 1970s, and in evening sales since 1994. This did not just indicate an increased acceptance by the public and therefore the market but was also a sign that economic success could come from moving beyond a focus on earlier art.[201] Many living artists were now so established that a private buyer would feel reassured without the advice of a gallery specialist. Most importantly, at that time the secondary market had caught up with the primary market in terms of sales. Sometimes so many works came to auction directly from the artist's studio that the sales became a barometer for 'emerging art'.[202] This encouraged investment and speculation; the traditional gap between primary and secondary market shrank to just a few years.[203]

In response, the gallery world began to diversify. Today, on one side there are a large number of small companies and on the other there are international chains modelled on the Gagosian enterprise, which aim to reach collectors on all continents through exhibitions.[204] Larry Gagosian's London competitor Charles Saatchi did not just rewrite art (market) history with his presentation of Young British Artists. His Internet platform saatchionline.com is also one of the most successful distribution channels between artists and collectors and registers hundreds of transactions every day.[205] In contrast, it took the auction houses another decade to harness the Internet for transactions as opposed to a presentation and information medium, after an initiative by Sotheby's from 1999 to 2003.

In 2004 the entire art market turned over a total of 24.4 billion euros.[206] Picasso's *Garcon à la pipe* became the first painting sold at auction to pass the one-hundred-million-dollar threshold, and the year also marked the first time that the total from an auction of contemporary work broke through the same barrier. At both events Tobias Meyer wielded the gavel.[207] The high point of the boom is considered to be an auction at Sotheby's that exclusively offered works by Damian Hirst in September 2008, in the middle of the global financial crisis.[208] The established framework was also challenged by the Phillips auction 'Carte Blanche' in November 2010, when the auction house offered an evening sale platform to the dealer Philippe Segalot, in which he could consign works and at the same time act as an agent for consignors and buyers.[209]

## 13  Tobias Meyer and the Rise of American Post-War Art

While Tobias Meyer wielded the gavel for Sotheby's, no superlative was omitted when referring to him. Not only was he the firm's principal auctioneer from 2004, but he also had been the firm's worldwide director for contemporary art since 1997. He wore 'two hats', as he once described it in conversation. He never claimed not to be competitive. The word does not just mean orientated towards competition; it also means setting and implementing standards. Once Meyer had determined that a work of art was of high quality, and at best unique, he wanted to get the price he deemed to be appropriate. To this end, he explored new avenues to reach potential buyers, which by then were established across the globe. On the rostrum all his energy was then channelled into the seductive charisma for which he became famous. He was able to maintain the level of tension over an entire evening – in English, German, and French, if necessary – like a consummate actor who keeps reeling in his audience. The show must go on; when a lot failed to sell, he shook off the setback with the elegance of the perfect gentleman smoothing over somebody else's faux pas.

His exceptional talent also sometimes earned him resentful accusations of forcing prices up from the rostrum. As if the job description of the auctioneer at the absolute top end of the market included any provisions to stifle the bidding! Unmitigated admiration earned him the moniker 'Adonis on the rostrum' – as if Meyer's undoubtedly attractive looks were somehow crucial in influencing buying decisions beyond the five-million-dollar limit! Admittedly, the almost balletic gracefulness of his movements, the impression of nearly playful ease he maintained in the middle of the fiercest bidding competitions, together with his calm voice, may all have contributed to drive bidders to their limit – possibly even on the telephones that are always connected to a saleroom and can often be crucial.

In any case, when Tobias Meyer appeared, the cameras started rolling. Even for members of the wider public who would not have dreamt of ever attending an auction, he had become the star of a distant world.

At heart, Tobias Meyer remains a traditional European. He is educated and polite without being obsequious; he is also highly focused and confident without being arrogant. Born in Frankfurt in 1963 into an academic family with an interest in art, he began his apprenticeship with a traditional art dealer in Vienna, where he also studied art history. At Christie's he learned the trade of the auctioneer, before moving to arch rival Sotheby's in 1992.

This first career move certainly demonstrates independence of mind, even while his professional future was still in the distance. A stellar rise came fast for Meyer, accompanied by a series of success stories, from record prices for Gerhard Richter and Jackson Pollock to the winning bid of $119.9 million obtained for a version of Edvard Munch's pastel *The Scream* in May 2012, making it the most expensive work at the time in auction history. The buyer of the pastel was, incidentally, the American investment billionaire and collector Leon Black, bidding by telephone. Meyer would have been aware that a strong commitment from Black was expected.

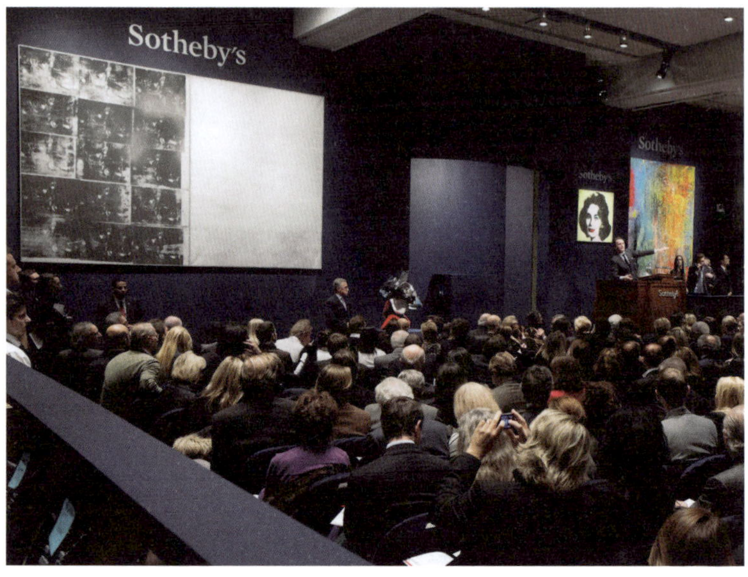

Tobias Meyer auctions Andy Warhol's *Silver Car Crash* for a hammer price of $94 million ($105.4 million with buyer's premium)

It was a real pleasure to watch Tobias Meyer work: Sotheby's evening sale audience in New York practically quivered with excitement in 2001, as he increased the bids on Max Beckmann's fantastic *Self-portrait with Horn* with passionate commitment. The record hammer price of $20.5 million for a key work of German Modernism still stands today. When the hammer fell, the legendary dealer Richard Feigen rose from his front row seat; he had successfully bought it on behalf of Ronald Lauder and his Neue Galerie for German and Austrian art in New York. Meyer was determined to reach the heretofore unimaginable twenty-million-dollar mark for a Beckman, not only because he wanted to win but because he felt that the price was appropriate and that it was in keeping with his own high appreciation of the work in art historical terms.

In May 2004 he also wanted to establish the singularity of *Garçon à la pipe*, created in 1905 at the cusp between Pablo Picasso's blue and rose periods. Of course he knew that he needed a bid of at least $90 million in order to break the magic one-hundred-million barrier, including the buyer's premium. He did it; he was able to knock down Picasso's charming boy for a final bid of $93 million (that is, $104.2 million with premium). While the audience was still catching its breath, he needed to keep his wits.

Some years later in a conversation in 2012 he explained the background; before the auction the dealer Larry Gagosian had announced his intention to bid above $70 million on behalf of a client. Gagosian started to bid – and then stopped. His mobile phone battery was empty. Meyer responded: 'Sir, do you need more time . . . ?' Gagosian grabbed the phone of the assistant next to him, redialled – and continued to bid. Meyer must have had nerves of steel, while the unsuspecting room was vibrating. In the end, Gagosian's client was not successful. Meyer however maintains silence about the winning bidder's identity. Absolute discretion is one of his much-appreciated characteristics.

He is also closely connected with the rise of American contemporary art at auction. In May 2007, his innovative approach managed to change the market for Mark Rothko. Previously, the artist had been appreciated mainly for his work in sombre tones, but Meyer produced a catalogue bound in white leather for *White Center (Yellow, Pink and Lavender on Rose)* of 1950 and presented it to potential clients from Hong Kong to Russia. He and Sotheby's had risked a guarantee of $40 million for the work, which had Rockefeller family provenance. He believed in the picture and he was proved right. At the auction, he remained almost entirely motionless on the rostrum as the bidding moved beyond $40 million. His minimalist on approach complemented the picture perfectly. The winning bid of $65 million came from the family of the Sheikh of Qatar and was the top price paid at auction for any contemporary art work at the time.

Meyer made his final appearance on the rostrum at Sotheby's on 13 November 2013, selling Andy Warhol's *Silver Car Crash (Double Disaster)* in New York. He increased the bids up to a hammer price of $94 million, a triumph not just for the grand master of Pop Art but also a personal one. Only ten days later it was announced that Meyer and Sotheby's would go their separate ways. We can only speculate about his reasons, which may be found in the competition between Sotheby's, a company listed on the US stock exchange, and the firm's arch rival, Christie's, owned by the French luxury market entrepreneur François Pinault. He may have felt that a listed company left him too little scope, also in financial terms.

One thing is certain: Tobias Meyer is not suited to be a marionette. He once said that he received the tool of his trade, the auctioneer's gavel, from Peter C. Wilson, Sotheby's celebrated head from 1958 to 1980. He will certainly never give away that souvenir, which he held in his hand while creating his own recognizable style. It remains to be seen if he will ever use it again on a public stage. In any case, his performance as an auctioneer has already made Meyer into a legend.

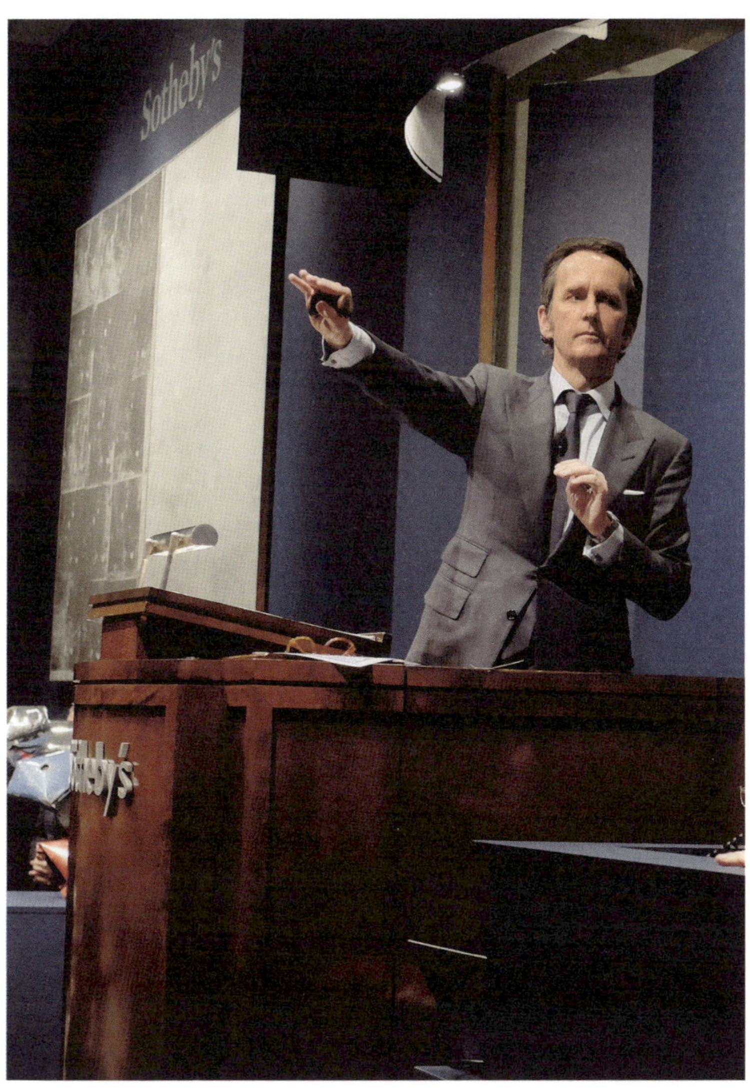

Tobias Meyer during his last evening auction at Sotheby's in New York
on 13 November 2013

## 14  New York 2013

During the years following the global financial crisis, the art market has performed a balancing act. On the one hand, the perception of art has been increasingly defined by the contemporary; on the other hand the art buyer has sought to combine an avant-garde and lifestyle experience with maximum financial reassurance. A global buying community has been activated and has proven  especially receptive to links between art and fashion, industrially produced luxury goods and prominent provenance, in addition to recognizing art as an alternative investment opportunity in times of low interest rates.[210]

Consequently demand has been especially high for post-war art. While the work is recent enough to convey intellectual glamour, it is also sufficiently accepted and tested. A freshly coined Anglo-American expression, 'trophy pictures', has been used to describe the so-called masterpieces that dominate art fairs and auctions, and above all influence public perception of these events. As we take this book press, prices seem to know hardly any bounds, and estimates as well as historic records continue to be exceeded regularly. The same is essentially true for Impressionist and modern works. However, between 2004 and 2012 their results have fallen behind those for post-war art, where demand has driven prices up by over 560 per cent.[211]

The buying community for masterpieces is truly global. Interest comes from China and Russia, Abu Dhabi and California. The international houses estimate that twenty times more active bidders participated in a sale in 2008 than in 1988. Since 2013 the single biggest market has been in China, though this relates largely to traditional Chinese art and antiques and much less to Chinese contemporary art.[212]

Chinese collectors who gained international influence however have been those who carefully observe global developments and began collecting Western art. Alongside collectors in Russia, India and South Korea, these tastemakers began by focusing on their own cultural heritage before branching out into other international developments and collecting trends. Even if the percentage of such bidders was small to begin with, they soon set records that drove the turnover of the global art market to 65.7 billion dollars in 2013.[213] The auction houses reached out to regions with promising buyers and created a global network, especially driven by Christie's, which has held auctions in Dubai from 2006 onwards and in Shanghai and Mumbai beginning in 2013. Citing its competitor's successful example, Sotheby's was reprimanded in public by its majority shareholder Daniel Loeb. Where the gavel does not travel, the Internet comes to the rescue. Many auction houses have broadcast their sales online for a number of years; Christie's decided in 2011 to introduce 'online-only' sales curated by specialists. Sotheby's responded in 2014 by launching a co-operation with eBay to turn that popular auction site's clients into buyers of fine art.

But the greatest expansion of the period took place in the core area of the art trade. Private sales have become a means for the auction houses to harness their knowledge of collecting desires and collection gaps in order to satisfy the consumers even outside the auction. Christie's, Sotheby's and Phillips now generate approximately a third of their income in private sales – and that must be the real revolution in the auction world![214]

## 14  Echoes of a Landmark Sale
## Jussi Pylkkänen on the Rostrum

When auctioneer Jussi Pylkkänen navigated the record-smashing $495,021,500 Post-War and Contemporary art evening sale at Christie's New York in May 2013, it seemed improbable at best that an even higher sum would be achieved just six months later, and then again in May 2014.

That November evening, Francis Bacon's iconic triptych *Three Studies of Lucian Freud* from 1969 sold to the Acquavella Galleries for an astounding $142,405,000, the highest price achieved for any work of art at auction.

Freud, outfitted in a white shirt with rolled-up sleeves and tight pants that show patches of bare skin from his shin, appears uneasy under Bacon's penetrating gaze. The fact that they were fast friends at that time, only later to become permanently estranged, added to the emotional intensity of the grand, three-panel composition, set behind glass.

Bidding opened at a stratospheric $80 million and quickly broke the hundred-million-dollar mark, escalating in five-million-dollar increments with bids from the floor and the long banks of telephones. It finally hammered at $127 million (before the buyer's premium).

The price of the Bacon eclipsed nineteenth- and earlier twentieth-century masterworks, including Edvard Munch's *The Scream* from

1895, which had sold at Sotheby's New York in May 2012 for a record
$119,922,500; Pablo Picasso's *Nude, Green leaves, and Bust* from 1932, which
had sold for a record $106,482,500 at Christie's New York in May 2010;
and Vincent van Gogh's *Portrait of Dr Gachet* from 1890, which had
fetched a record $82.5 million at Christie's New York in May 1990.

That high-water mark for *Dr Gachet* held its own until May 2004,
when Picasso's *Garcon à la Pipe* from 1905, sold from the collection of
Mr and Mrs John Hay Whitney, became the first one-hundred-million-dollar painting to sell at auction, realizing $104.2 million at Sothe-
by's New York.

During the bid- and record-busting sale at Christie's in November
2013, other records were set as well, including Jeff Koons's *Balloon Dog
(Orange)* sculpture from 1994–2000, which brought $58,405,000, and
Christopher Wool's boldly graphic text painting, *Apocalypse Now* from
1988, which went to the Van de Weghe Gallery for $26,485,000. It crushed
the previous £4.9/$7.7 million Wool high set at Christie's London in
February 2012.

The Bacon triptych that evening in November 2013 was one of three
lots exceeding $50 million, while eleven made over $20 million and
sixteen hurdled over $10 million.

Remarkably, or so it seems in retrospect, a decade earlier, the November 2003 evening sale at Christie's in that same category made a
then respectable $62 million. It was led by Mark Rothko's darkly lumi-
nous abstraction, *Untitled* from 1963, which sold for $7,175,500. Alexan-
der Calder's sixteen-foot-high painted metal stabile, *Untitled* from 1968,
made a then record $5,831,500.

Six months later, in May 2004, Sotheby's Post-War and Contemporary evening sale broke the one-hundred-million-dollar barrier for the
first time.

Fast forward again to the same Rockefeller Center salesroom in May 2014 and witness Pylkkänen's third consecutive record-breaking sale in New York for any category, this time achieving a massive $744,944,000 for the sixty-eight lots that sold. Sitting across from Pylkkänen over lunch the next afternoon, I could tell that the strenuous evening had taken a temporary toll on Christie's president of Europe, most apparent in his English accented voice, which had an unusually raspy edge to it. After ordering a bowl of carrot soup to soothe his scratchy throat, Pylkkänen began to analyze the previous evening's results, taking pains to emphasise the rational movement behind the sky-high figures.

'There's been a real consolidation and acceptance of the price levels set in May 2013 and that became a kind of jump-off point to where we are now. You can tell by the depth of bidding for masterworks in subsequent sales that collectors have grown to become very comfortable at those levels.'

For those unfamiliar with Pylkkänen's fast-paced yet meticulous auctioneering style, the newcomer's seemingly easy-going delivery masked a tensile like strength in both strategy behind-the-scenes knowledge of both the artworks and potential bidders, even the ones screened behind the telephones. That style had been exclusively in evidence at the major London auctions until November 2012, when he took over the gavel in New York from Christopher Burge, Christie's star auctioneer who commanded the Manhattan salerooms with extraordinary élan for some twenty-three years.

That recent May evening with Pylkkänen on the rostrum was also a statistician's dream, with eleven works selling for over $20 million, and of those, five made over $40 million each. Ten artist records were established, and among that cavalcade, Joseph Cornell's extraordinary and patently surreal *Medici Slot Machine* from 1943 – a wood box con-

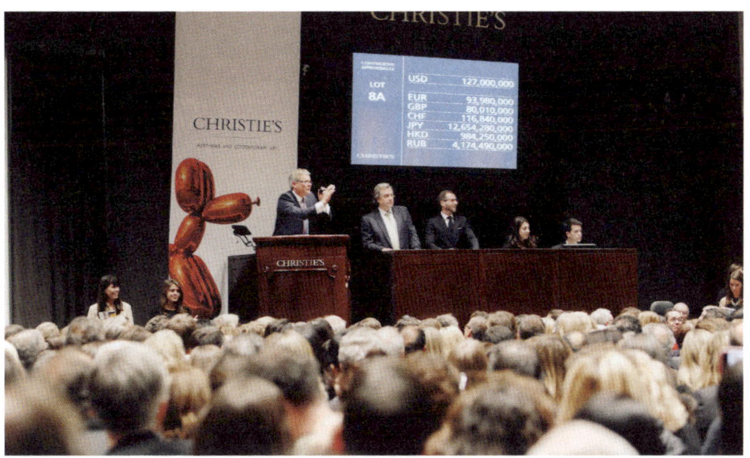


The record hammer price of $127 million ($142.4 million with buyer's premium) is achieved for a painting on 12 November 2013

struction comprised of glass, printed paper, including the reproduction of Pinturicchio's *Portrait of a Young Boy* of circa 1495–1500, collage, metal, mirror and marbles – sold for $7,781,000 (estimate $2.5–3.5 million). It was from the estate of the late and great Chicago collecting couple Edwin and Lindy Bergman, who made major gifts to the Art Institute of Chicago during their lifetimes.

Another standout from the Bergman trove was Alexander Calder's fantastic hanging mobile, *Poisson Volant* (Flying fish) from 1957, which made a record $25,925,000 (estimate $9–12 million).

The evening was built in part on such estate collections and other rare-to-market works, such as Jean-Michel Basquiat's *Untitled* from 1981, featuring a crowned, nude warrior figure armed with a sword and arrows and set against a blazing orange and yellow background branded with Basquiat's unique street language and scrawl-like mark making.

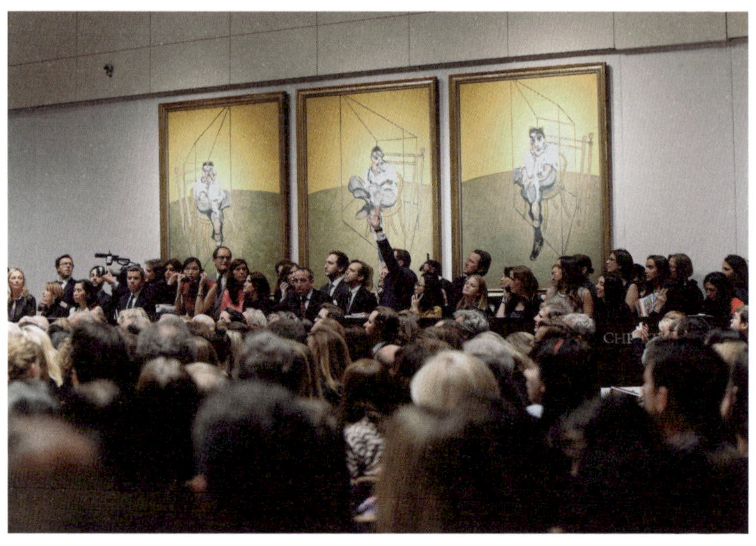

The auction of Francis Bacon's *Three Studies of Lucian Freud*, 1969, oil on canvas, November 12, 2013, Christie's, New York

It fetched $34,885,000 (estimate $20–30 million). The late Washington-area collector Anita Reiner acquired the painting in 1982 from the Annina Nosei Gallery in New York, the dealer who first launched Basquiat in SoHo.

Another Reiner estate offering, Robert Gober's ghostly, twenty-inch-high sculpture, *The Silent Sink* from 1984, handmade in plaster, wire lath, wood and semi-gloss enamel paint, sold to George Economou Collection curator Skarlet Smatana for a record $4,197,000 (estimate $2–3 million). Like many other works in the sale, the Gober sink carried world-class museum credentials and had been included in the 2007 Gober retrospective at the Schaulager in Basel. Going through the alphabet of blue chip masters, Joan Mitchell's large-scale, lyrical and colour-charged

*Untitled* canvas from 1960, the year she permanently settled in France, sold for a record $11,925,000 (estimate $6–9 million). It also became the most expensive work sold at auction by a woman artist.

Barnett Newman's iconic abstraction, *Black Fire I* from 1961, a majestic, one-hundred-and-fourteen-by-eighty-four-inch painting that had been on extended loan at the Philadelphia Museum of Art from 1985 to 2014, sold for a record-shattering $84,165,000 (estimate on request), literally doubling the Newman record.

The anonymous seller acquired the painting from London's Mayor Gallery in 1975 for around $150,000 – no doubt a whopping sum at the time and barely a year after it had sold at Sotheby's Parke Bernet in New York for $95,000, according to gallery owner James Mayor, who sold the painting to the consignor.

The fact that the owner harboured the painting in a great American museum for so many years and allowed it to be loaned in major exhibitions around the globe certainly burnished its allure in this market's deep-pocketed quest for unassailable quality.

The epoch-making evening for acquiring masterpieces at massive prices was not restricted to just pretty pictures. This was evidenced by Andy Warhol's four-panel *Race Riot* from 1964, based on an appropriated black-and-white photograph taken in Birmingham, Alabama in 1963 by Charles Moore during the height of the civil rights movement, and featuring a defenseless black man being attacked by two police dogs.

It is widely considered the most politically charged subject among Warhol's Death and Disaster paintings and was included in the Warhol retrospective at the Museum of Modern Art in 1989, two years after the artist's death. It sold to the Gagosian Gallery for $62,885,000 (estimate on request). The sixty-by-sixty-six-inch acrylic and silkscreen ink on linen last sold at Christie's New York in November 1992 for $570,000 (estimate $600–800,000); it was obviously a very different point in time for the art market.

The May 2014 auction was a signature, double-feature evening for Warhol. The twenty-by-sixteen-inch *White Marilyn* from 1962 was also on sale, signed by the artist and dedicated to his then dealer Eleanor Ward of the Stable Gallery to mark his first solo New York show there in November 1962, where identically sized works of the screen goddess in different background colours were on offer at $250 apiece.

The petite painting ignited a bidding war that went on for almost ten minutes. At $34 million, and after agreeably splitting a bid from one of the tenacious telephone bidders, auctioneer Pylkkänen broke the tension with a deadpan question, 'Would anyone else like to come in?', causing laughter and a much needed jolt of energy to keep the room humming. It helped drive the final price skyward to $41,045,000 (estimate $12–18 million).

'The reality of the art market today', said the auctioneer, 'is that the new buyers are buying art based on the quality of the artist and the importance of the work. It's all about masterpieces because the masterpieces can engage people from across the globe. What we've seen in the last few years, particularly in the American artists of the 1950s and 1960s, they've become global painters in a way that Picasso and Monet were.'

Remarking on how fast this post-war market has moved, Pylkkänen observed, 'I remember a year ago, there were six works or so that sold for over twenty million dollars during the week of Post-War and Contemporary sales. As the auctioneer, I wondered when a work at twenty million came up, how many bidders I would have. That no longer goes through my mind.'

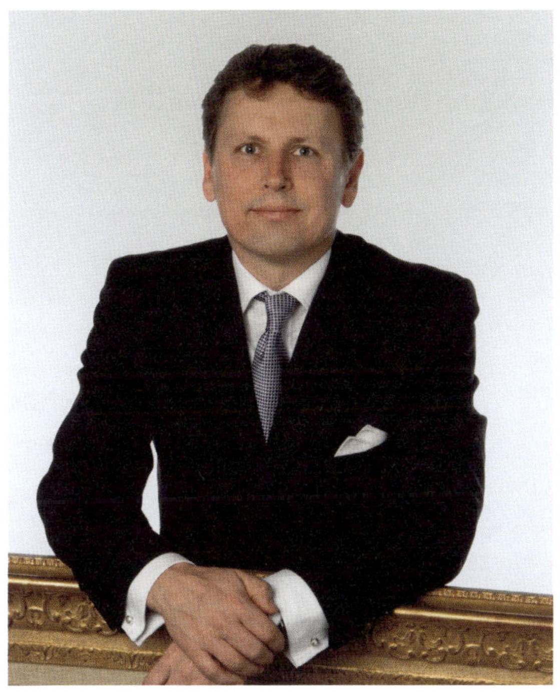

Auctioneer Jussi Pylkkänen

## 15  The Day-to-day Business of Auctioneering

The personalities presented in this book are outstanding protagonists in the art world and its traditions, as are the authors who describe them. People make history, and they are the focus of attention here. Extensive background on the day-to-day aspects of the business is available elsewhere. The summary that follows is simply intended to satisfy those who cannot wait to investigate further.

No country in the world has legal requirements for the domestic art trade, other than the requisite trading license.[215] Such professional titles as gallery owner, art dealer and art adviser are not subject to any regulations, protection or control. The execution of auctions is legally regulated however; the auctioneer is therefore the only participant in the art market whose activities must comply with a legal framework. The reason for this special treatment is the peculiarity of the auction, where the knockdown of the auctioneer's gavel transfers ownership.[216]

Consequently the auctioneer presents himself vis-à-vis the bidder community as a neutral middleman rather than as a representative of the owner of the goods to be sold. This special position is protected internationally by regulations designed to prevent the exploitation of mutual trust. These legal provisions control the auction process and follow its chronology. Typical stipulations cover the existence of written instructions by the seller for the auction sale. The conditions of business and the catalogue of objects to be sold both need to be pub-

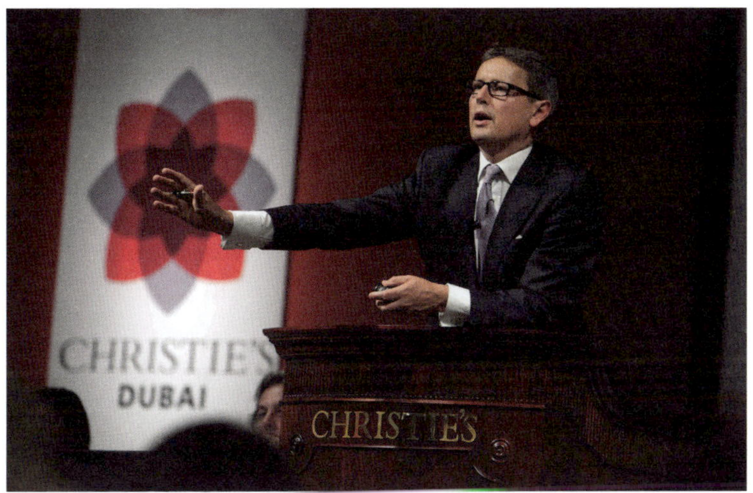

Jussi Pylkkänen on the Rostrum in Dubai 2013

lished, and there is a requirement that objects be made accessible to potential bidders. The auctioneer has every freedom in accepting bids; the lot can only be knocked down however when the winning bid is repeated three times and no higher bid comes forward. Each winning bid must be recorded in writing. When the hammer is knocked down, the regulations concerning the auction process cease to apply, and subsequent activities such as an after-sale are no longer covered by any special provisions.

By the way, it is strictly forbidden to offer alcoholic beverages for the duration of the auction.

During an auction the buyers offer competing bids in public; these bids are successively raised. (This applies to the so-called 'English auction', in contrast to the so-called 'Dutch auction', which follows a successive lowering of the price, or the 'silent auction', where bids are made

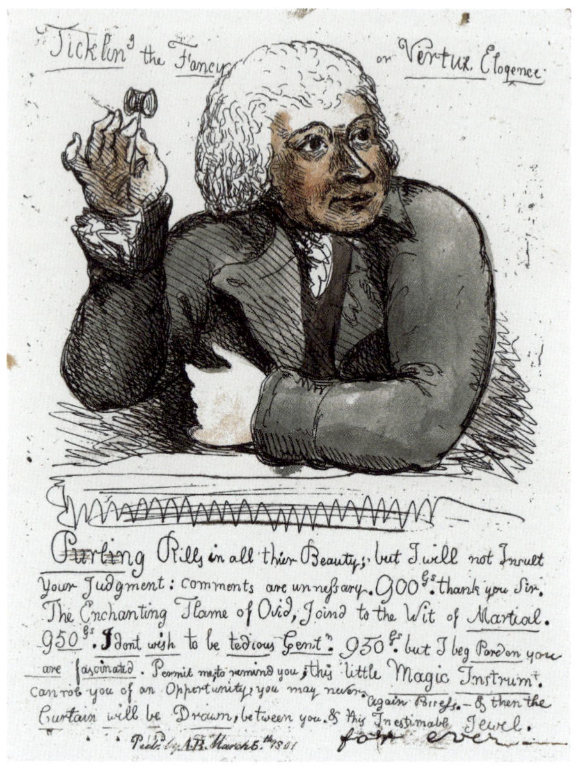


Caricature of James Christie, 'Ticklin' the fancy', signed 'A.R.'
and dated 5 March 1801

in writing only and remain hidden.) The seller is able to influence the
starting point for the bidding through a minimum price, the reserve.
Each bidder can bid multiple times. The auctioneer begins with the first
lot, which is shown at the same time either in the room or as an illustration. Bids are raised by 10 per cent, and the highest bidder wins the
lot, once the auctioneer has called out the winning bid three times

before knocking it down. The current status of bidding is displayed on an electronic board, as well as converted into the main global currencies. (This invention was Roman Norbert Ketterer's and was subsequently adopted by all large auction houses.)[217]

The actual sale occurs not with the knockdown of the gavel but through the auctioneer's calling out 'sold', '*adjugé*', '*verkauft,*' etcetera. The knockdown is merely an audible signal indicating the closure of one lot before opening the next; it provides the rhythm of the sale. The gavel is also comparable to a sceptre, used by the auctioneer to 'bless' the sale and direct the events in the saleroom.

The room bidder on the opposite side is legitimised by his paddle, which displays his bidder number. No bidder is allowed in the room without a paddle, to avoid bidding without having first provided veri-fiable personal details. The bidding itself is done by hand signals, which become more discreet with the increasing experience of the bidder. His objective must be to avoid signalling his interest to his competitors too early. However, the urban myth of an unintended purchase through head-scratching or waving is highly improbable. Any auctioneer will double-check at the slightest doubt.[218]

The successful bidder number is called out only at the knockdown. If there is no buyer, the auctioneer will say 'passed', '*passons*', or '*durch-gefallen*'.[219] Auction room etiquette demands that no heads should be turned in the audience to see the winning bidder. The professional bid-der will therefore be found at the back of the room. Since he has already inspected the lots during the preview he does not need a front-row seat to see the desired object.

The auctioneer opens the bidding at roughly half the estimate. This is meant to encourage a bidding war and lead to higher prices. Until the reserve price is reached, the auctioneer can use fictitious 'chandelier bids' to call out the next increments. This practice can annoy newcomers, since it creates the illusion of interest in the lot. From the perspective of the seller, however, the practice merely protects his interest in reaching the reserve price at which he is prepared to sell. Chandelier bids are therefore bids carried out by the auctioneer on behalf of the consignor.[220] If the reserve is not reached, the consignor 'buys' his own lot. In Anglo-American usage, an unsold lot is 'bought in' ('BI' for short).[221]

The auctioneer must stand 'on the right foot'. This does not refer to his posture on the rostrum but to his following the correct sequence of bids. He knows the increments that drive the auction, and the reserve price. If he has a commission bid in the auctioneer's book, he must pace himself so that the absentee bidder can win the lot, provided there is no higher bid in the room. If he is 'bidding against the chandelier', he must seek to obtain a real bid upon reaching the reserve. If the final chandelier bid is on the reserve, the lot remains unsold, even though there may have been a potentially winning bid in the room.[222]

When the lot is sold, the auctioneer must accept no more bids – in theory. If a client made a mistake and would like to continue bidding, the temptation is great to reopen the lot in order to raise the price further. It frequently happens that a lot is reopened even at a later stage. The international houses however follow the unwritten rule that a lot can only be reopened as long as the following lot has not yet been called.

Typically, between fifty and sixty lots are sold per hour. The weaker the demand, the slower the auction becomes, which allows time for indecisive bidders to make up their minds. On the other hand, extensive bidding wars can also sometimes slow down a sale.

A good atmosphere in the saleroom is essential for the success of an auction. This puts the personality of the auctioneer centre stage, as

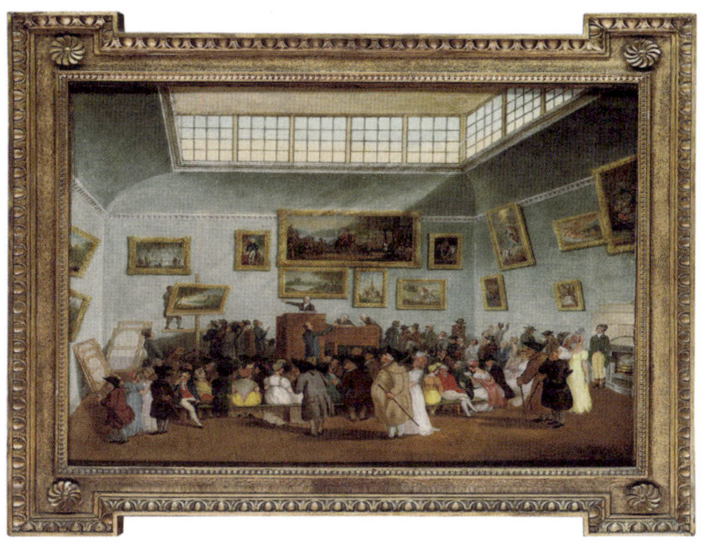

English painter, after Thomas Rowlandson, *Christie's Auction Rooms*, ca. 1800, oil on canvas, 62 × 75 cm

nowadays he must not just be a skilful salesman but also a masterly entertainer. Emotionalising the process is part of what mark's the auction's evolution from wholesaler to retail business, driven by the auction houses since the 1970s.[223] Art auctions used to be simply an intermediary business, generally serving as the biggest supply chain for the trade. Only top end auctions at the traditional London houses were also regarded from the beginning as a social event and often attracted private collectors who bought directly. When famous collectors appeared on the scene, such as the American industrial magnates around 1900, the presence of private clients increased, without yet challenging the predominance of the trade.[224]

Auctioneers of that era reported that it was their job to call out incremental prices and take bids. No entertainment, no seduction – the clientele were professional buyers who knew exactly how much they could spend to ensure their subsequent profit margin. Accordingly, no estimates were printed in the catalogue. Only the art market crisis of the 1970s and modern sales and procurement planning brought about a change in mentality. Since turnover cannot be increased through increasing sales of objects, the only way to do so is through expanding demand in order to raise the price level. This required a greater auction involvement of direct customers. An increase in competition drives prices upwards, especially as direct customers are not obliged to build a profit margin into their bidding level. This in turn had a marked influence on the role of the auctioneer. The more successful he is in entertaining and tempting the bidders, the higher the result of the sale will be.

Today, the most important skill of the auctioneer is to generate the desire to buy, be it mild or an all-encompassing passion. This will produce bidding wars, with some clients appearing to bid just because they enjoy the activity. Many private collectors find satisfaction in having a bidding opponent. This is not just about confirming one's choice of object; there is also the element of a power struggle. Only two bidders remain at the end of an auction, and each will hold up the sale and keep the audience on tenterhooks while they make up their mind whether to bid once more.[225]

The competition for a desirable object is a veritable battle, which can be fought to the bitter end. The gavel coming down on the winning bid is the moment of victory. The opponent could not keep up; he is beaten and will have to be called upon to prove his worth again. Nowhere else is so much money spent in such a short period of time: the saleroom is the perfect stage for self-dramatisation. Sometimes the successful bidder can be left with a feeling of remorse for having over-paid – since nobody else was ready to go that high. This is referred to as 'the winner's curse'. The only comfort is that of having won just by one bid – after all, the defeated under-bidder was prepared to pay almost as much.[226] The disinterested observer will come to the unemotional con-clusion that the under-bidder knows as much as the buyer but is perhaps a little less wealthy.

If the object is very expensive, or the bidding war especially long and hard, the victory of the winning bid is often celebrated by a round of resounding applause in the room. The question is what is applauded: the ability of the auctioneer or the courage of the victorious bidder?[227] Roman Norbert Ketterer once rewarded the bidder in an unusual way: he handed a white carnation from a vase by the rostrum to each winning contestant.[228] The auctioneer himself cannot display too much elation after the knockdown. Later on, the press office will handle the public-ity for a new record price, which is only whispered in the saleroom. The auctioneer has to convey the confidence that the auction price is at the right level for the object. The disinterested spectator remains unmoved, because at that moment he joins the ranks of the cognoscenti, who know that the price was right.

Generally, the atmosphere in the saleroom comes to life when a critical mass is reached, which also guarantees publicity for the victo-rious bid. It may be regretted that more and more high prices are cur-rently achieved through bidding on the telephone or via the Internet. If the trend continues, the event status of the live auction could be chal-lenged, even though the telephone bid increases the price in the same way as a floor bid.

These days the art world generally converges on the saleroom only during the spectacular evening sales for fine art held in London, New

York and Hong Kong. During the day sales, or auctions of smaller and less highly priced collecting areas, the number of bidders in the room has been sinking drastically, especially since the introduction of Internet bidding. Sometimes there are more staff members – on the rostrum and at the telephones – than there are clients in the room. An even more dramatic development can be observed during Country House sales in the provinces; even though the viewing may be attended by hundreds, since it offers a weekend diversion and sometimes a look behind the scenes in a stately home, the sale itself can take place in a near-empty room, with the auctioneer taking only telephone and internet bids.

The bidder from outside the room is an invisible competitor for those inside; he cannot be assessed.[229] This puts the auctioneer in a difficult position: he can try to tempt a room bidder, but he can only communicate indirectly with the telephone bidder, who is represented by the staff member speaking with him. The employee communicates the status of bids from the room and if required raises his hand to bid on behalf of the client. It is therefore helpful for the auction atmosphere when the most important clients are seated in the saleroom. The distribution of seats requires military precision, and the auctioneer is of course provided with a seating plan so that he can easily locate the main stakeholders and is less likely to miss a bid.[230]

In this context auction houses welcome the current trend to bid via the Internet, since this allows more direct forms of communication between the bidder and the auctioneer, who can be viewed on the bidder's screen. Nonetheless, the auctioneer in such a format can sometimes feel like a television game show host, as two bidders battle for victory in front of a selected 'studio audience', while the wider public watches from home, their reactions inscrutable. Moreover, while the Internet client may decide to join the bidding at any time, his entrance will

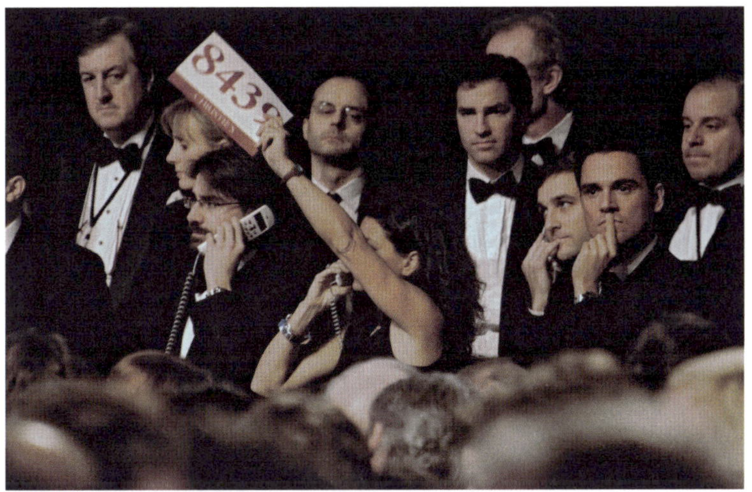

Bids being taken over the phone at an evening auction

generally take the auctioneer by surprise; whereas the auctioneer is skilled at detecting the first signs of nervousness in a room bidder, the Internet auction in its current form hardly conveys this personal electricity.

It remains to be seen whether new technology such as measuring an Internet bidder's eye activity or mouse movement might provide the auctioneers of the future with a digital prognosis for their invisible audience. (This kind of technology is already used by the automobile industry, for example in driver alert systems.) In addition, a solution may be found for the problem that the auctioneer can only ever engage with the first Internet bidder to come through. If there are several room bidders on the same increment – if, that is, they are bidding virtually simultaneously – he can at least gauge the depth of interest from the unsuccessful bids he decides not to select. If however an Internet bidder

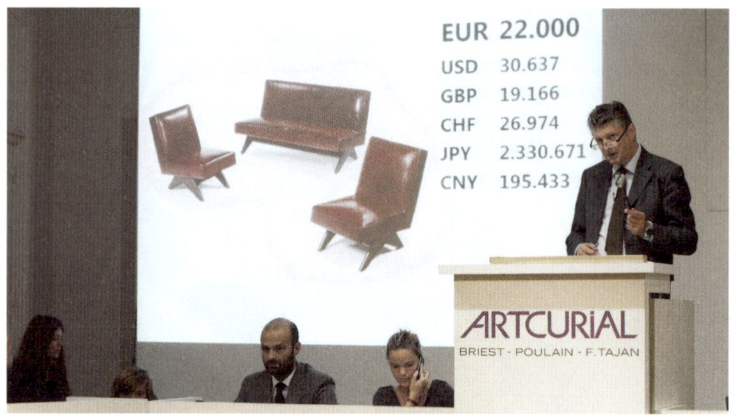



Amie Siegel, *Provenance*, 2013, HD video, 40 min., colour/sound (still)

clicks his mouse just a nanosecond too late, the bid is lost and will not even be transmitted to the saleroom. One hopes that technological advances may one day resolve this issue.

All the different options for absentee bidding have of course increased the demands on the auctioneer's ability to entertain. Why should the client come to the saleroom if not to see a live show? Meanwhile, a professional client such as a dealer can remain at his own premises and go about his business as usual. Should a lot be called up in which he has already registered interest, he will be alerted by a discreet sound signal on his computer. This practice takes away the saleroom's traditional function as a meeting point and discussion forum for enthusiasts of a particular art movement, including collectors, journalists and dealers. It is conceivable that the Internet auction will eventually replace the live auction. If that happens, and the auctioneer starts selling to a virtual audience only, his or her talents will then surely be judged more than ever on the basis of external media-friendly qualities.

One hopes however that the medium will also be able to convey something of the spellbinding atmosphere generated by a room full of passionate bidders and coolly interested onlookers.

## 16    Circuit: *Provenance*

While living in Berlin on an artist's residency, I made a film concerned with the remainders of former East Germany, *DDR/DDR* (2008). One sequence follows the journey of a moulded plastic chair from a former socialist apartment block to a contemporary flea market, where it is bought and placed on display in a hip Berlin furniture store – then spotted, bought again and sent on a container ship across the ocean, finally landing, marked-up considerably, in an upscale Tribeca design store.

The star of that montage was a common East German plastic chair design – a Communist version of the classic Verner Panton. A few years later I came upon the same chair in an auction catalogue. It had entered the market as my film imaginatively predicted. A quotidian object in one context assumed the valuation of a rarefied, fetishised object in another. Photographed on white seamless for the auction catalogue, the chair looked amused, as if aware of the irony of its situation: captured from the wild and resold in the very (western European) marketplace its original communist designers and fabricators would have shunned.

Leafing further through the auction catalogue, I opened to a spread of teak and cane chairs from Chandigarh, India, designed by Le Corbusier and Pierre Jeanneret. I recalled a friend's photographs from a trip to Chandigarh, the city Le Corbusier made from scratch: the monumental government building complex, university, city sectors, streetlamps, sewer covers, and furniture oddly piled up on roof terraces and in office hallways in the photographs. Looking at the catalogue I realised, those piles were likely the furniture designed by Le Corbusier and Pierre Jeanneret for Chandigarh. Further research revealed thousands of these pieces – chairs, settees, daybeds, desks, benches, bookcases, stools – were originally made on site, in Chandigarh, from the Swiss architects' roughly one hundred designs, differently adapted and executed. And now the Chandigarh furniture was being auctioned globally, appearing in the showrooms of Christie's, Sotheby's, Bonhams, Philips, Artcurial, Wright 20th Century. An immense trafficking in the furniture was underway.

Starting from this chance encounter, I created a large-scale work, *Provenance* (2013). The film installation begins with the Chandigarh furniture in situ, in the homes of western collectors who bought the furniture and – like a document detailing the lineage of ownership – moves backwards from there to the auction of the furniture in North America and Europe, the preview exhibitions, photography for the auction catalogues, backwards to the furniture's 'restoration', shipping across the ocean and, finally, returning to India with the original furniture in the Le Corbusier buildings. This epic project unspooled across cities, countries, the middle of the Mediterranean (one collector had the furniture on a mega-yacht) and oceans, unfolding a vast network of connections over time. The film focused on the furniture – often eclipsing humans – and eschewed dialogue, creating an uncanny, anthropomorphic enactment of diaspora as the furniture changed hands.

For over a year, I filmed in collector's homes and the auction houses in Europe and North America, tracking the Chandigarh pieces. While shooting in the preview areas and auction rooms featuring design – staged and spot-lit furniture and objects – I would occasionally drift away from the film crew and find myself in a different part of the auction house, one that previewed a sale of silver, jewels or, more often than not, art. There I recognised a certain haphazard aspect to the installation – the lawlessness of multiple objects brought together by the motive of *resale.* For an artist such as myself, who works intensely with montage – bringing together shots, locations, otherwise disparate images and ideas – the unbridled juxtapositions of the secondary market of art disturbed me, traveling the divide between object and beholder as a jarring jumble of things, of commodities.

But there was another feeling, one which crept up on me like a chill as I happened unexpectedly upon these oddly hung salons of paintings and sculptures, a kind of gloomy cold that would descend further as I passed through each room: the slow realisation that I had in another way crossed over, ferried now into the Hades-like afterlife of objects, the in-between place art goes before being reborn to its new owners, its next life. Viewers, collectors, lovers of art can go there with the ease of their attachments – an event to pass the time, or to search for new wares, investments, passions – but for artists, witnessing this liminal space can be an unsettling feeling. The merchants of art descend upon the pickings, rather like Hitchcock's birds circling above their prey. (There's a reason why the director included an auction scene in *North by Northwest*, set in a hotel – Chicago's Ambassador West – itself a space of transience.) And one observes in a kind of horror, watching hundreds of artworks change hands in an evening, a sight that should perhaps not be experienced first-hand by artists, seeming to cut against an order of things where art was once resold only after the death of the artist, and the auction was a kind of belated stage of arrival, one that is not simultaneous to the artist's life, out there in the world, still making work, but *after.*

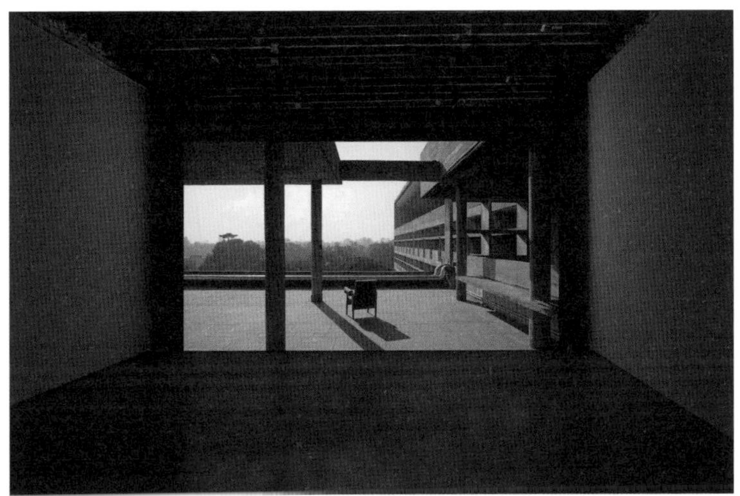

Amie Siegel, *Provenance*, 2013, HD video, 40 min., colour/sound (still)

The first auction catalogue I studied at length was, ironically, a sale of the collection of a well-known 1960s New York artist, offered by a venerable auction house. The heavy tome was filled with disparate worldly objects, hinting at the artist's affinities with Modernism's universalist conceptions, evidence of his late blooming interest in Buddhism and Asian artefacts, oddly co-mingling with Arts and Crafts furniture and masks from Borneo. The collection also included drawings, paintings and objects by the artist's peers, suggesting a lifetime of intimate trading, and provided carefully staged context for the artist's own work for the sake of the auction sale, casting value back on his objects.-

The catalogue seemed at first a potential source of comfort, inspiration – glimpses of what an artist's life might look like after years of work – but instead of stimulation, a sense of depression set in after

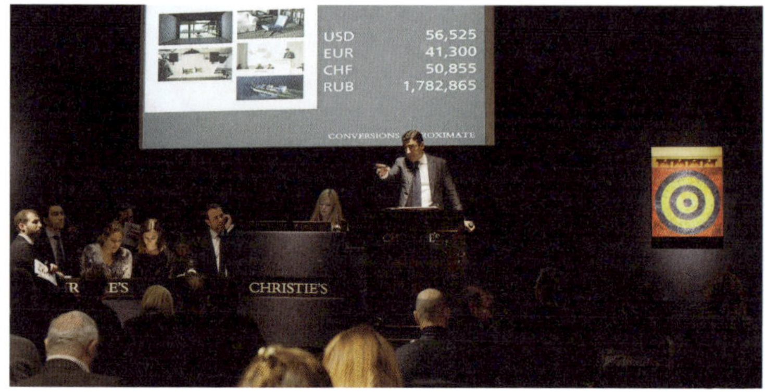


Amie Siegel, *Provenance*, 2013, HD video, 40 min., colour/sound (still)

studying its pages. The evidence on display of a life replete with the cultural accumulations of the successful artist was suddenly just that, and a mere fleeting stretch on the longer continuum of objects and their movements. Things are gathered but for a moment before they are disassembled and then re-absorbed into different gatherings, with new owners and adjacencies. This molecular structure of cultural artefacts combining and separating is barely visible from our limited temporal perspective, occupying – as we do – several quick scenes across a century. Individual owners are ephemeral, interim custodians. Meanwhile the object moves on, fickle, through vast expanses of history, subject to motivations of profit, speculation, theft, exploitation, the whims of fashion, taste, pedagogy, pathologies of the encyclopedic, of completion as well as profound and inexplicable attachment.

It was while filming in London that I committed to an idea that had been growing in my mind since the start of *Provenance*. That morning we had just finished filming in Notting Hill and Kensington, and I had been at a lunch afterwards up on Bishops Avenue in the home of collectors who own my work. The movement from the homes of collectors of the Chandigarh furniture to collectors of my own work was a bit jarring. After the lunch, while walking in nearby Hampstead Heath, I stopped in at Kenwood House, a former stately home and now a public museum. There I came upon a work by William Hogarth, *Taste in High Life* (1742), a forerunner to his satiric popular print series *Marriage-à-la-mode*. The painting depicts an aristocratic family surrounded by their accumulated things; a monkey stands centre frame, examining a list of recent purchases at auction by the family.

This trenchant work by Hogarth reminded me of the long tradition of landed, wealthy westerners acquiring cultural objects, particularly those from the Orient, parlaying the patina of the exotic into their own lives. I was particularly impressed by the self reflexive humour of Lord Iveagh, who acquired this work for Kenwood House, then his home, to mirror his own family's existence.

The uncomfortable feeling of closeness to the thing I was filming – collectors acquiring the treasures of mid-century Western design (layered with the patina of the East, of India) and the collectors who acquire my own work – as well as the meta-gesture of the Hogarth collector, combined into a notion: that *Provenance*, the film I was making, should itself be brought to auction. I would film the auction of my film, which would then become another work, to be exhibited together with *Provenance* thereafter.

On 19 October 2013 the first edition of *Provenance* was offered in the Post-War and Contemporary sale at Christie's, London, only one week after the close of the work's premiere exhibition at Simon Preston Gallery, New York. This was the last available copy of the work, the remaining editions having been bought in the weeks prior. *Provenance* sold at Christie's for £52,500.

The resulting film, *Lot 248* depicts the Christie's preview exhibition and heated auction room bidding contest for *Provenance*. The entire ensemble of works, including *Proof,* the Christie's catalogue spread from the auction of *Provenance*, embedded in Lucite like a frozen quarry, is currently on view at the Metropolitan Museum of Art, New York through January 2015 in the acquisition exhibition 'Amie Siegel: Provenance'.

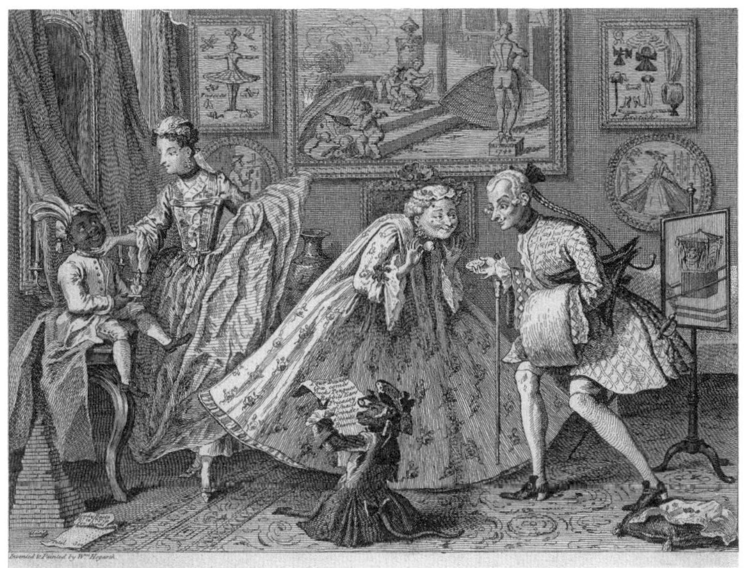

William Hogarth, *Taste in High Life*, 1742, oil on canvas, 63 × 75 cm (shown here in an engraving by Samuel Phillips, 1798), Victoria & Albert Museum, London

## 17 A Bid for Love
## *The Heir* by Vita Sackville-West

Who, the non-initiate may ask, actually attends art auctions? Not forced sales and other unpleasant aberrations of the business, but the beautiful auctions, the ones that take place in beautiful venues and offer beautiful objects whose written provenance is as rarefied as an entry in the Almanach de Gotha. Surely these are impassioned people, connoisseurs, famous individuals who nonetheless shun celebrity and whose names are whispered in awe. Such shimmering stars can only be recognised in the firmament by people who actually know the constellations: Great Bear… Venus… Unicorn. And what are the others? Surely one of them is a peacock? Even if we do not have the faintest idea about people and stars or their statistical probability of attending auctions, we may certainly hazard the guess that those who attend have a lot going for them.

Peregrine Chase is none of the above. He has nothing, and certainly nothing going for him either. He is a hybrid without desire, a human entity lacking sex or character. No passion, no substance. At the beginning of his extraordinary story, in the year 1922, he is far removed from involvement with the world of beautiful auctions. What would he do there? Chase is poor. In the unsparing and unceremonious words of his creator, the writer Vita Sackville-West, he is hardworking in a cheerless fashion, a backwater bachelor insurance salesman, a nobody, who smokes too much, eats too little and does not know how to coax any pleasure out of life. Delight, desire and delectation are as alien to him as a mirage, a promenade in the park, or indeed the stars in the infinite sky. He is too timid for all this, and too pale.

It seems bizarre that Peregrine Chase is a member – well, maybe not a member but an associate by name – of a family going back hundreds of years, and that this name ultimately entitles him to inherit a centuries-old estate. He himself finds this embarrassing. Peregrine Chase is helpless in facing the complicated genetic skulduggery that has led to the inheritance. He never knew the imperious aunt who bequeathed him the legacy. Her body lying in state disconcerts him even more, as does Blackboys with its manor house, associated servants, smug-looking peacocks – yes, peacocks! – which roam the park in flocks, and the highly indebted estate with its tenants. And if that were not enough, there is adroit Mr Nutley, the lawyer, notary and executor of the deceased. He quite intends to take charge of the heir's affairs and sets about doing so in an expeditious, meddling and assertive manner. Nutley's hour has finally come: the hour of the auction.

This is because Peregrine Chase, lacking both passion and wherewithal, has no choice but to consign everything to auction as soon as he has consigned his aunt to the grave. Never mind the coat-of-arms, the name or the five hundred years of respectability. He was not brought up to deal with this and cannot even imagine doing so. Why should he? He has no money to fund the indebted estate, the mortgaged house and the costly gardens, and certainly no money to feed the greedy peacocks. He is not used to enjoying a stroll in this, has no imagination to fill rooms, gardens and grounds with life.

The auction in which the novella culminates is both a necessary and sadly also ominous action for Peregrine Chase. Even though this is not meant to be a forced sale, for Chase it has none of the glamour of

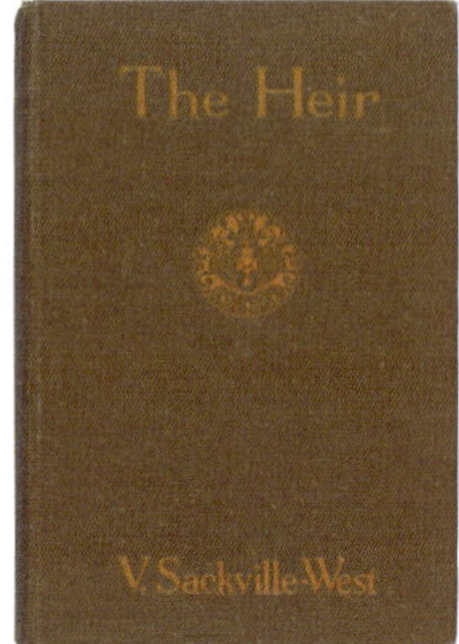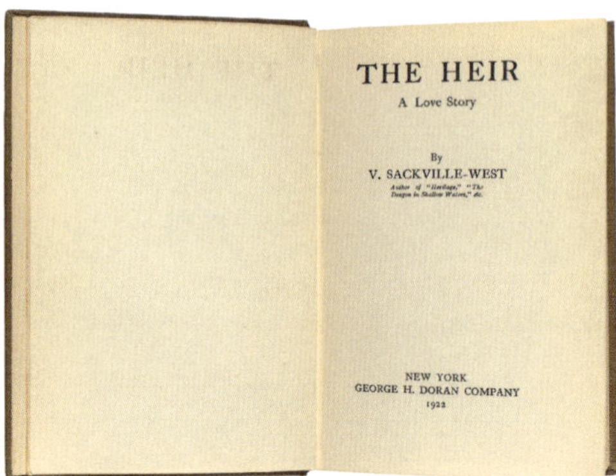


Vita Sackville West, *The Heir*, first edition, published in New York
by George H. Doran, 1922

auction events where personages with accomplished taste, great names
and even greater bank balances float through rooms filled with treasures, apparently for no other reason than to reinforce the eternal cliché
of a blissful life at the top. . . . Even if Peregrine Chase had had the audacity to imagine the auction as a magic moment in his life, he would
never have conceived of it as an epiphany leading to a veritable explosion. As he explores the house and gardens for the first time, admiring
the birds of paradise mirrored in stellar constellations, he cannot even
begin to guess that he himself is a bird of paradise among heirs in the
literary world.

Auctions, auctioneers and auction houses are rare in literary fiction.
There is not even a small niche allocated to them, unlike in cinema,
where auctions are used to signal a particular ambience, an established
aesthetic and social background. This is a world full of beautiful objects,
populated by satiated and not always beautiful people. Auctions in film
have ample dramatic potential: secrets, meticulous provenances, sur-

prise offers, unexpected disputes, emotions of all shades and register. They contain a wealth of species and set the scene for a wide variety of characters – much like the world of diplomacy – and they maintain the illusion that no tragedies are possible in such a context; everything offered for sale is delicious, precious, luxurious.

Apparently writers rarely frequent places where property and goods come under the hammer. Perhaps they also labour under the prejudice that the auction venue is exclusively glamorous and therefore unsuited to any serious narrative. Or perhaps literature, unlike film, is first and foremost a medium of the inner voice, of the invisible, and that auctions display objects that do not require such a voice. Perhaps the people, who bid or consign are then simply forgotten, while it might be both exciting and revealing to give them a voice. The objects, however, are magnificent before the camera, imparting an enchanted ambience for the surrounding cast of characters.

An obvious example is the film adaptation of Josephine Hart's best-selling novel *Damage* from 1991. The novel's protagonist, Anna Barton, is a journalist, but film director Louis Malle made her an art historian and diplomat's daughter (played by Juliette Binoche) who works in a well-known auction house in London's Bond Street. With her air of immaculate elegance and a mystique enhanced by general opulence, she carries the flair of a rarefied world into her private and intimate life. In the film, Anna wears this like a personal attribute. Her polish makes her sexual greed appear even wilder, all the more intoxicating and un-controlled. If we compare the book and the film, we cannot but appreciate the elements that work in the film but not on paper, and vice versa.

Ian Fleming's short story *The Property of a Lady*, published posthumously in the 1960s, is mostly remembered for its connection to a Bond film; the auction scene it describes became a set piece in *Octopussy*, released in 1983. In recent years, a few literary protagonists who work in auction houses have appeared,[231] but the auction itself remains extremely rare as a literary subject.[232]

One bestseller furnishes an exception. Leanne Shapton's *Important Artifacts and Personal Property from the Collection of Lenore Doolan and Harold Morris, Including Books, Street Fashion, and Jewelry* (2009) is neither a novel nor a short story; it is a fictitious auction catalogue. The objects under the hammer tell much about the characters who assembled them and the love they shared. This is touching, not least because this book demonstrates our human connection to objects and the fact that these objects generally outlast our loves and indeed ourselves. Leanne Shapton is in fact not a writer but an artist. Her oeuvre is closer to the work of Sophie Calle, who creates books mixing auto-fictitious elements with an artist's invention. Both artists pursue the process of creating evolving ideas rather than telling a linear narrative. As fascinating as Shapton's fictitious auction catalogue seems, it is not helpful in bridging the gap between literature and the auction business. For the fine arts are often more daring in their subject matter than literature.

What, then, inspired Vita Sackville-West to use an auction not merely as a subject of fiction, but even as the culmination of her 1922 novella *The Heir?* She wrote that it was the shock of witnessing the attitude of an acquaintance, a wealthy banker from South America, who was considering buying an English country estate. Her protagonist is pure fiction however, and Sackville-West, the grande dame of the British landed gentry, invests him with all her convictions. Inherited property is far more significant than mere material possession. History and personal experiences both with and in a house, the gardens and the land itself are spellbinding. This enchantment may, at best, shape and

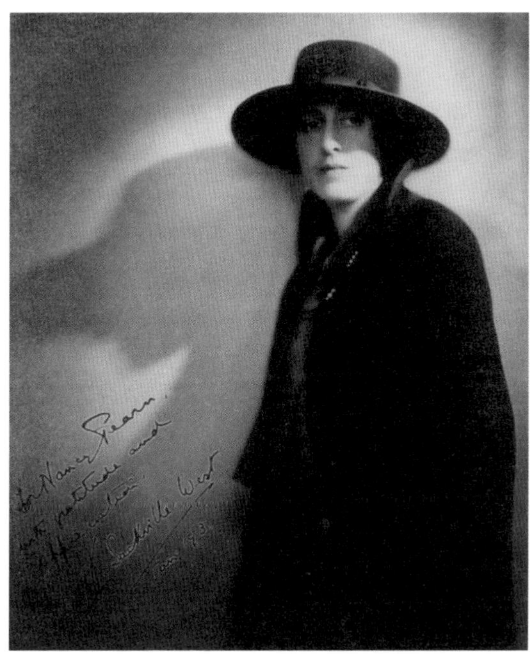

Portrait of Vita Sackville West, 1931, Photograph, 31 × 25 cm

develop a personality beyond tangible reality. Only untalented and ignorant materialists such as the lawyer Mr Nutley can see gains in the sale of such a property. They simply confuse *value* with profane *profit*.

For his part, Peregrine Chase knows nothing of the possibility of an *éducation sentimentale*. He has not been taught to value atmosphere or become part of it, and he has no trouble letting himself be persuaded by Nutley. But then a few weeks pass, and the heir takes some tentative steps into the unknown. Unwittingly he begins to enjoy the new terrain. He feeds the peacocks in the park, accompanied by the dog of the testatrix. He talks with the tenants. He brings flowers from the gardens into

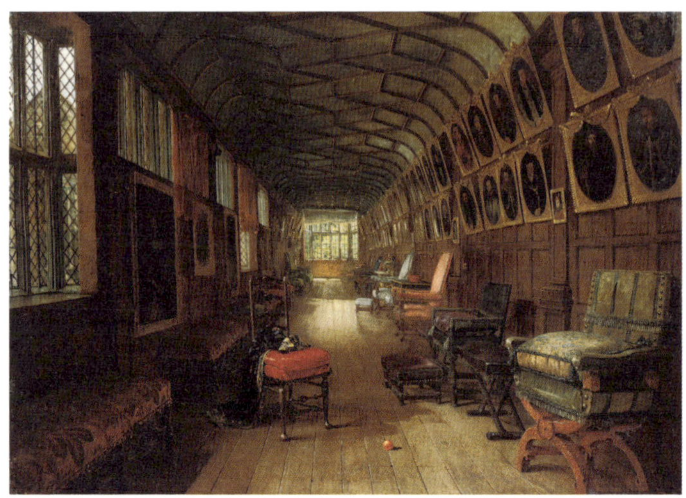

Louise Rayner, *The Brown Gallery*, *Knole*, oil on canvas, 51 × 69 cm

the house. He adopts habits that are suited to his inheritance but have nothing to do with his former life. At night he watches the stars, listens to the sounds and breathes the scent of trees and plants. This is not love at first sight, for Chase does not know what love is. He is enchanted without knowing it. Then he returns to his insurance, and Nutley takes the helm – or rather, the gavel.

Nobody expects Chase to actually make an appearance at the sale, least of all Chase himself. When he does enter the room, few of those present know who he is, not even the auctioneer. Then there is a sensation. Sackville-West takes the reader on an accelerated tour of this unimposing character's belated éducation *sentimentale*. Peregrine Chase has a lightning epiphany. Step by step he reveals his state of mind. The strangers are surprised, believe the man is drunk – for Chase is bidding. Nutley is beside himself. He tries to convince the auctioneer that a madman has entered the bidding. But the timid Mr Chase outdoes himself. Through and during the auction he realises that with this house he has found his true self. He has what he always unwittingly wanted, and now he shouts out bid after bid as he takes a stand in the fray. This is his battle. For the first time in his life Peregrine Chase has something for which he will and can bid. Not the house, not the garden, not the estate. He bids for love. He is in love! The auction is his chance to bid for happiness. And he wins! For the first time he really and truly lives! What a perfectly successful éducation *sentimentale.*

## 18  Best Offers
## The Top 12 Auctioneering Scenes in Feature Films

Hors concours:

**CONVERSATION PIECE**

Director: Luchino Visconti

With Burt Lancaster, Helmut Berger, Silvana Mangano

Italy, 1974

'Brilliant!' is the first word spoken by Burt Lancaster in the opening scene of Luchino Visconti's masterful *Conversation Piece*. He is holding a magnifying glass over a nineteenth-century picture. Dealers from the Blanchard gallery would like to offload it on him for £3,500. The auction houses Christie's and Sotheby's are mentioned in the same scene, but without any visible auction scene (contrary to my recollection). This is a film about the beautiful old world versus the new world (with its boundless levels of elegance as well as arrogance), and the inevitable failure that results. Visconti's direction is so flawless that even forty years later the iconic names being mentioned easily lead to an association with an imaginary auction scene. Visconti knew exactly why he placed his protagonist among art, dealers and auctioneers right at the beginning of his film. As a Marxist aristocrat who himself owned a substantial art collection, he was well aware that this world would be the most conclusive setting for conveying a character's personality, status and background.

12. **THE MAGIC CHRISTIAN**
Director: Joseph McGrath
With Ringo Starr, Peter Sellers, John Cleese, Roman Polanski, Raquel Welch, Christopher Lee, Yul Brynner
United Kingdom, 1969

This film is a loose adaptation of a book of the same title by Terry Southern. It proved to be a gigantic flop at the box office despite the huge star presence of Peter Sellers, Ringo Starr, Raquel Welch, and Yul Brynner (in drag!). Even the hip '68 generation found it to be over-the-top and of no significance whatsoever. The film does have one mildly entertaining auction scene set at Sotheby's. A Rembrandt portrait goes from ten thousand up to thirty thousand pounds ('Thirty – thousand – pounds? *Shit!* I beg your pardon!' 'I do beg your pardon.') Then the nose is cut out with a pair of scissors right in front of the auctioneer. Not even great stars can save a truly dreadful script. This film would have been left unsold at auction. Fair warning.

11. **MONEY TALKS**
Director: Bratt Ratner
With Charlie Sheen, Chris Tucker
USA, 1997

This comedy is not great cinema but rather television material with a decent Barry White soundtrack. In this buddy movie, an Afro-American con man (Chris Tucker) seeks help and protection from a white TV journalist (Charlie Sheen). Notably, after an hour or so of fairly clichéd material, the film then culminates in what is possibly the most vulgar auction scene in film history. The lot to be sold is Cary Grant's car from the film *North by Northwest*. Almost the entire repertory of finger movement is employed, from the finger against the cheek and the straight middle finger into the cheek to the raised arm. We find ourselves longing for Hitchcock's cinema and the elegance of the 1950s, anything to rescue us from the cheap gaudiness of the 1990s. This is as painful as having to compare the most beautiful women of the heyday of Italian cinema, actresses like Lucia Bose, Silvana Mangano, and Monica Vitti, with the 'tutti frutti girls' of Silvio Berlusconi's bunga bunga parties. A film in free fall!

## 10. OCTOPUSSY

Director: John Glen
With Roger Moore, Louis Jourdan, Maud Adams
United Kingdom, 1983

It is no secret that, despite its suggestive title, the thirteenth Bond film was not one of the best in the 007 series. Perhaps it is because the sets were not designed by Ken Adams, whose drawings and photographs fetch top prices at auction today. Or was it maybe the lack of great action scenes? Faye Dunaway was originally supposed to be the Bond girl, but even Faye Dunaway would not have rescued the film. For our eyes only!

The auction of a Fabergé egg is taken from one of the sources for the script, Ian Fleming's short story *The Property of a Lady*. Precisely this egg is identified in London as a fake at the beginning of the film. James Bond visits Sotheby's together with the expert to look into the background for the forgery. This is where the original is to be sold, and Bond surreptitiously swaps it with the fake. The highest bidder is a shady Arab prince known for illegal art dealings and receiving stolen goods. Bond believes this is an important lead and is instructed to follow the man.

Apart from this, the auction room scene is not unfortunately very memorable except for the fact that Roger Moore plays it so confidently. It does capture a poised and elegant atmosphere typical of the genre and the time, but that hardly makes *Octopussy* any more interesting.

## 9. TRANCE

Director: Danny Boyle
With Vincent Cassel
United Kingdom, 2013

Danny Boyle rewrote film history with *Trainspotting* (1996) and *Slum Dog Millionaire* (2008). Probably his most ambitious and costly production however has been *Trance*, which Boyle wrote in parallel to preparing the gigantic opening ceremony at the 2013 London Olympic Games. This is by no means the best film ever, even though we get to witness the imaginary auction of a magnificent Rembrandt right in the opening scene. As it turns out, the picture has already been stolen; only an empty frame remains on the easel. Voice over: 'It used to be: everyone could steal a painting. There was no need for a gun! All you needed were strong nerves and a car. But these days are gone. We have bag searches and magnetic alarms, and silent scanners and x-ray machines and cameras'. Then, in the middle of all this commentary the robbers arrive: 'This is a robbery!' they yell, and the auctioneer can only stammer 'No piece of art is worth a human life!' Once again, it's every man for himself, as chaos ensues.

In another scene, Goya's *Witches in the Air* is being sold, while in the basement three gangsters (including Vincent Cassel) grab some guns and prepare to create utter mayhem. They enter the saleroom just as the auction reaches its climax at a bid of £27 million for the Rembrandt. 'It is imperative not to panic! Remember, do not be a hero!' The gangsters flee over the rooftops with the picture. As soon as they unwrap it they realise they were taken in: just an empty frame remains.

The main female character starts out as a relatively mousy therapist. But she has hypnotic abilities and can manipulate all and everything. She turns out to be a femme fatale. Her presence drags the film increasingly towards carnality while the plot veers towards the absurd. Danny Boyle's bewitchingly rich imagery can be overwhelming for the viewer, but it can also stand in the way of following the sequence of events. This film belies Liberace's favourite saying: 'Too much of a good thing can be wonderful!' But Danny Boyle certainly does make the most of his attractive leading man Vincent Cassel. Even if you cannot buy a Rembrandt or a Goya in *Trance*, at least there is the French body beautiful!

## 8. MICKEY BLUE EYES

Director: Kelly Makin

With Hugh Grant, Jeann Tripplethorn, James Fox, James Caan

USA, 1999

*Mickey Blue Eyes* also starts right in the middle of an auction sale, with Hugh Grant as the auctioneer on the rostrum. When lot 85 comes up, however, an assistant informs him that the picture has not been delivered in time. Hugh Grant quips to the packed room 'We feel as stupid as I'm sure we look.'

Later he locks horns with a consignor of paintings who yet again delivered weeks too late. The consignor: 'You gonna sign, or do I take it all back?' The auctioneer: 'That's your response to this?' The consignor: 'All right guys, load it up.' Finally Grant signs and unloading takes place. 'I think every auction house in New York has these delivery hiccups.' And a passer-by: 'Sotheby's doesn't seem to.' Although the film is set in America, thanks to Hugh Grant's wonderfully British accent and the excellent dialogue one feels in England, where a sense of humour is as essential to daily life as a line of coke up the nose of a high-flying Hollywood producer. (Sadly, this is all too obvious in most of today's mainstream films, but that is yet another story. . .)

An elderly lady asks Grant: 'How much is this one?' 'On this, the reserve is 30,000 dollars, I think.' Granny is already rummaging in her bag to look for the dough. Grant: 'Do you have much experience when it comes to buying art?' Granny: 'But I hear it can be a great investment!' 'If you are looking for something beautiful to put on your wall, you might like to think about a mirror.'

And finally, there is a slightly absurd third auction house scene, where the Mafia is bidding on a ghastly picture against the very same old lady. The price goes from $80,000 to $115,000 because she has lost a hearing aid and misses the auctioneer's 'Ha' signal that had been agreed beforehand. That is one way of losing a lot of money. But the man with the gavel finally speeds up so much that the lady is saved. And so the film reaches a surprising happy ending, in spite of a protagonist who is not really dead after all.


## 7. SHERLOCK HOLMES: A GAME OF SHADOWS
Director: Guy Ritchie
With Robert Downey Jr., Jude Law
United Kingdom, 2009

There is an impeccably staged auction scene right at the beginning of Guy Ritchie's second Sherlock Holmes film, *A Game of Shadows*. While an Egyptian stone sarcophagus is sold, a woman gives a parcel to an elderly gentleman. Sherlock Holmes, who has been following the woman, arrives just in time to remove the bomb in the parcel from the room, together with a letter the gentleman was carrying. To clear the saleroom, Holmes enters the bidding on one lot and then stages an arson attack on a tapestry. He then hurls the parcel bomb into the stone sarcophagus, where it explodes. Guy Ritchie is too clever a director not to have studied every detail of the scene in Hitchcock's *North by Northwest*. However, he did not just imitate Hitch. Ritchie attempts to apply precise stage direction and lots of humour to generate a maximum of suspense, so that the film does not lose the momentum built up through elaborately choreographed action scenes full of daring ellipses. The auction provides a slightly mechanical background to the action, until the auctioneer calls out 'One million pounds!' Sherlock Holmes starts the fire and coolly shouts 'Oh, by the way, there is a fire!' Cary Grant could not have delivered it better for Hitchcock.


## 6. SEX AND THE CITY

Director: Michael Patrick King
With Sarah Jessica Parker
USA, 2008


Needless to say, the entire feverish trashiness of the eponymous TV the preceded it had an impact on the film *Sex and the City*. It is impossible to ignore a winning brand, and the laws of commerce have to be followed. As even the second scene in the film is set at an auction house, the set-up is as exaggerated and 'clownish' as can be expected.

The camera shows Christie's rooms at Rockefeller Center, with an off-screen comment: 'It was a rare occasion that brought all types of women together. Once she was a waitress turned model turned actress turned billionaire's girlfriend, until she found herself turned out after ten years.' Now is the time for revenge! She consigns all the jewellery to auction that her sugar daddy ever gave her. When a flower ring comes up ('This flower ring is the essence of me!'), the unusually nouveau riche saleroom clientele reveals itself: 'Hey, she's bidding for somebody on the phone!' 'That's not fair.' 'Bitch!', 'The gloves are off.' Then one of them shouts 'Fifty fucking thousand dollars!' The director would have liked to have given her paddle no. 69, which Christie's naturally does not provide. Instead, they gave her no. 969! It may be somehow more 'pure', or could it be wishful thinking for our future love life? 'The more the merrier?'

Afterwards, there are complaints: 'I thought this auction would be fun, but it's kind of sad!' Late insight or nature's silent vengeance, when the woman sees her man only as a mobile wallet, and the entire consumer paradise New York becomes her lover?


## 5. MOUSEHUNT

Director: Gore Verbinski
With Nathan Lane, Christopher Walken
USA, 1997


This madcap comedy is an early example of Gore Verbinski's particular strengths: slapstick with formidable imagery, effervescent humour, the wildest action scenes possible and furious acting direction. Is goes without saying that all this is wildly over the top and entirely an acquired taste, especially bearing in mind how much money Verbinski's comedies rake in. His latest productions such as the *Pirates of the Caribbean* trilogy are among the most successful films of all times.

*Mousehunt* has one of the longest auction scenes in cinema, and it is at the heart of the film. The craziness is almost on par with the Marx Brothers. A house is being auctioned, and the house is inhabited by a mouse. The small creature drives the auctioneer to distraction, until he tries to kill it with his gavel on the rostrum in full view of the entire room. No such luck! The mouse ends up in the cleavage of a female bidder. To liberate it, her neighbour reaches unabashedly deep into her décolleté, whereupon the lady seated next to her would like to share in these ups and downs and blatantly manoeuvres the man's hand in the same indecent position on herself. All this, while the auction continues.

Later on, the mouse seeks refuge in a man's trousers, where a male colleague tries to address the problem, which again comes across as terribly indecent and compromising. Finally the mouse tries to hide in a gigantic hairpiece, which leads to a desperate attempt to drive the daring little animal out of this nest with a blast of fire. This in turn requires water. To cut a long story short, at the end the entire house is under water, and when the main door opens, the action scenes in *Titanic* come to mind. No wonder that the actual auction remains a backdrop. Almost unnoticed during the hullaballoo, the price has gone up from one million to five million dollars.

## 4. FIRST WIVES CLUB

Director: Hugh Wilson

With Sarah Jessica Parker, Bette Midler, Goldie Hawn, Diane Keaton

USA, 1996

'Revenge is sweet', is the shared motto of three women on whose faces a tough and exhausting social life has already left its marks. They plan to bring financial and social ruin on their men, since every one of them has disgraced himself though infidelity. During a magnificent auction scene, the three ladies are supported by the inimitable Maggie Smith playing a grand society lady. Her outfit goes perfectly with the saleroom interior, as if she were part of its inventory. Out of loyalty to her three friends as well as the desire to take revenge on the wealthy airhead sitting next to her, she entices her neighbour into placing insanely high bids. With phrases like 'Jackie O. had one just like it!' the stakes are raised and raised. 'This sofa was on the cover of *Architectural Digest*', is

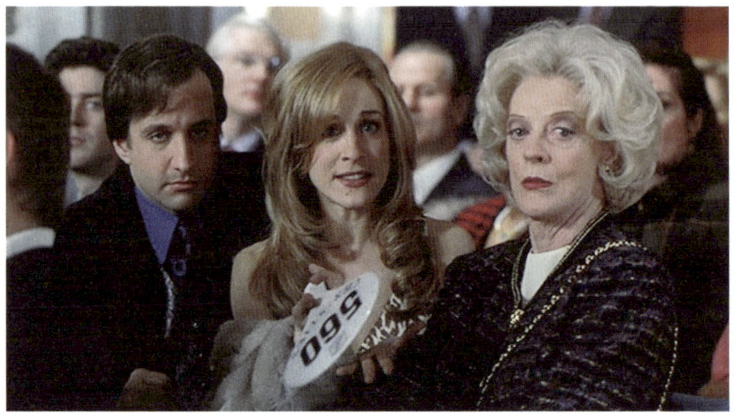

Film still from The First Wives Club, 1996

one of the lines that serves to reinvigorate the temporarily stalled bidding.

We can easily imagine the same pointed remarks being made in one of today's salerooms. Even within the audience, all that glitters is certainly not gold. There are fakes under as well as across from the auctioneer's hammer.

Later on, when the dumb blonde comes home to her sugar daddy, she has to account for herself: He: 'Fifty thousand dollars for a used carpet? A *used* carpet?' She: 'Jesus, I want a lifestyle! With some ambiance and some classic, eternal good taste.' He: 'But not for over fifty thousand dollars.' She (sulking): 'I can leave if you like.' And so he starts to unzip her dress and thinks that the Lamborghini she bought during her auction shopping spree for $300,000 was really rather a bargain. Better sex through Christie's?

### 3. THE ADDAMS FAMILY

Director: Barry Sonnenfeld

With Raul Julia, Angelica Huston, Christina Ricci

USA, 1994

The auction scene in this 1994 blockbuster is brief but all the more preposterous for its brevity. The two main characters Morticia (Angelica Huston) and Gomez (Raul Julia) are bidding successfully on an object that they themselves have donated. They could not care less what the price will be, as they are engrossed only in each other and cannot keep their hands off each other, even during the auction. Morticia's ecstatic screams blend seamlessly into the traffic noise of LA traffic, leading practically from intra-auction intercourse to interchange at the main junction in Los Angeles. Hollywood shows how it is done. Only the inimitable Cher, who was predestined for such moments and would have liked to have played the female lead, could have produced a similarly delightful and histrionic scene with its unique brand of caricature.

### 2. HOW TO STEAL A MILLION

Director: William Wyler

With Audrey Hepburn, Peter O'Toole, Hugh Griffith and contributions from Givenchy, Cartier, and Coiffure Alexandre

USA, 1966

Set in the milieu of the rich, the beautiful, and the charming rogue, this heist comedy film immediately provides a considerable level of comfort. The first take captures the auctioneer's ivory gavel mid-move-

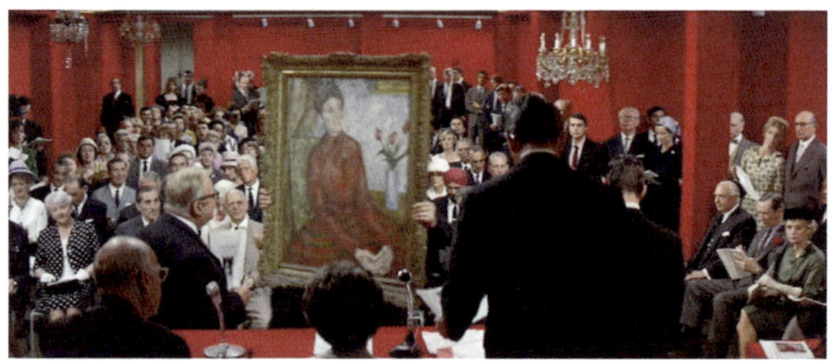

Film still from *How to Steal a Million*, 1966

ment, as it seals the winning bid for a picture. Next we see a superb Cézanne, starting at $200,000. There is an accomplished forger in the room, Monsieur Bonnet (Eli Wallach). Telephone lines connect to New York and London, as the bids start to rise quickly. At $240,000 the white lapdog of an otherwise unremarkable lady barks a bid, but the scene continues. Only at $270,000 do we see Audrey Hepburn in a white killer outfit by Givenchy, driving her red cabriolet – welcome to the real world. Later on she hears that a dealer bought the Cézanne for $515,000. She clearly feels uneasy, because her father is a highly talented forger who churns out Cézannes and Van Goghs by the dozen. In order to imitate the perfect patina, he rubs original dust from Van Gogh's studio onto the canvas. Together with Stanley Donen's *Charade*, Wyler's *How to Steal a Million* is one of the most ingenious and entertaining heist comedies of the 1960s. Directing this sophisticated comedy in Paris must have been a walk in the park for the man who handled the monumental epic *Ben Hur*. To quote the title of another Audrey Hepburn comedy: 'Paris when it sizzles!'

## 1. NORTH BY NORTHWEST

Director: Alfred Hitchcock
With Cary Grant, James Mason, Eva Maria Saint
USA, 1959


*North by Northwest* has clearly got to be the winner of the hit parade of auction house scenes in feature films! While Visconti's *Conversation Piece* was the ultimate chamber play, Alfred Hitchcock's *North by Northwest* also filmed a key scene in a so-called set piece, using the 'Magnitude of VistaVision' format, as referenced so nicely in the trailer. The auction house scene, which is practically compulsory for any film student, has it all. Of course even a normal auction has an element of high voltage suspense, but Hitchcock does not leave it at that. He uses the auction to pull out a whole bag of tricks. The hero (Cary Grant) confidently strides into the auction house. Close-up from behind: his menacing testosterone-fuelled choking hand at the neck of the requisite Hitchcock blonde (Eva Maria Saint). The camera pulls back: the two protagonists (James Mason as the villain and of course Cary Grant) are engaged in what is probably the coolest duel with words in film history. Here you feel that Hitchcock was British. An American director would hardly have had the audacity to reduce his main actors to their pure physical beauty in this manner. They are puppets on a string. The auction continues in the background, while James Mason manages to operate on two entirely different levels, proceeding to bid while fending off Cary Grant's severe verbal attacks. Great lines are dropped such as 'I didn't realise you were an art collector. I thought you just collected corpses.' Remarks that bring a Barbara Kruger tableau to mind. The film takes care of the iconic images anyway.

There is one further auction scene, where Grant bids the entire sum of $13 for a picture in order to save his skin. An old lady bidder quips dryly: ' You're no fake. You are a genuine idiot!' But as viewers, we know who the real idiot is here: it is the high-handed collector, who could never be an object of sexual desire for Mr Thornhill (Cary Grant). Nice for the audience. We are in the cinema. Illusions are allowed! This is Hitch showing his wonderfully subversive side.

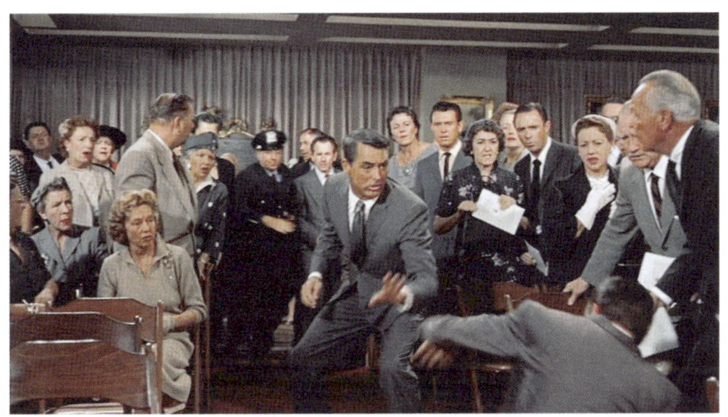

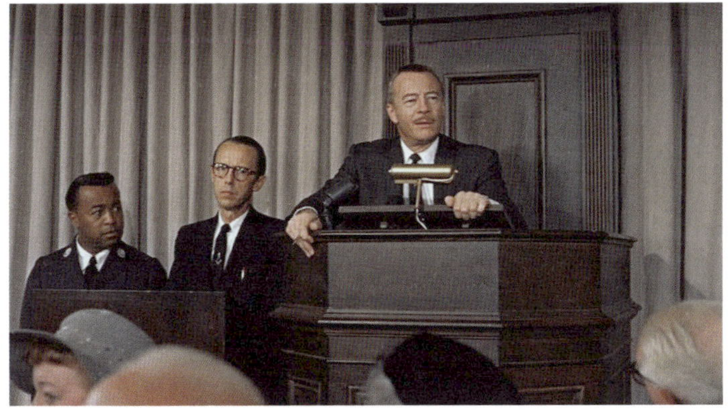

Film stills from *North by Northwest*, 1959

# Endnotes



## A Cultural History of the Art Auction in 14 Portraits

1 TEFAF, *The International Art Market 2013* (Maastricht, 2014).

2 Aspirin Cardion, www.youtube.com/watch?v=3eoyZCLjwfU (accessed September 5, 2014).


## 1  London 1766

3 Adolph Donath, *Der Kunstsammler: Psychologie des Kunstsammelns* (Berlin, 1923), p. 54.

4 Manfred Reitz, *Berühmte Kunstsammler* (Frankfurt and Leipzig, 1998), p. 76.

5 Hannelore Sachs, *Sammler und Mäzene: Von der Entwicklung des Kunstsammelns von der Antike bis zur Gegenwart* (Leipzig, 1971), pp. 82–83; Hans Peter Thurn, *Der Kunsthändler: Wandlungen eines Berufes* (Munich, 1994), p. 59.

6 Burton Fredericksen and Julia Armstrong, *Verzeichnis der Gemälde im deutschsprachigen Raum vor 1800* (Munich, 2002), p. 7.

7 Gerald Reitlinger, *The Economics of Taste* vol. 1: *The Rise and Fall of Picture Prices 1760–1960* (London, 1961), p. 3.

8 Robert Lacey, *Sotheby's: Bidding for Class* (Boston, 1998), pp. 38ff.

9 Nichols Powell, *Christie's* (Paris, 1999), pp. 9–10.

10 Thurn 1994 (see note 5), p. 67.

11 Reitlinger 1961 (see note 7), pp. XI, 5


## 1  James Christie: The Power of Place, Promotion and Personality

12 I am most grateful for the kind assistance given in preparing this essay by Christie's archivist, Lynda Mcleod.

13 *Gentleman's Magazine*, vol. 73, part 2 (1803), p. 1098. Notice of the 1760 sale was tracked down by Joseph Friedman in the *Daily Advertiser*, 24 July 1760. Thomas Mortimer, *The Universal Director; or, the Nobleman and Gentleman's*

*true guide to the Masters and Professors of the liberal and polite arts and sciences, and of the mechanic arts, manufactures . . . established in London and Westminster, and their environs . . .* (London, 1763), pp. 92–93.

14   John Greenwood (ca.1729–1792) in Leicester Square was probably Christie's main competitor in the 1780s, and Skinner and Dyke in Berners Street thereafter.

15   Today the site of the Institute of Directors, opposite Royal Opera Arcade.

16   Today part of the site of the Royal Automobile Club.

17   *Public Advertiser*, 12 December 1768. William Whitley, *Artists and Their Friends in England* (London, 1928) vol. 1, pp. 186–87.

18   On the present site of Waterloo Place. In March 1773 Christie hired Lyceum Gallery in the Strand, and in the first quarter of 1774 some sale catalogues refer to sales taking place at another Christie 'Great Room', in St Alban's Street, St James's Square, part of Market Lane off the north side of Pall Mall, opposite no.125. They were used by the Free Society of Artists for their exhibitions in 1775–76. (There were also several high class brothels in the area, and in the early 1780s one of London's most sensational attractions was to be found in the central section of Schomberg House: James Graham's notorious Temple of Hymen housing a 'Celestial Bed', designed to cure sexual problems.)

19   Hugh Brigstocke, *William Buchanan and the Nineteenth-Century Art Trade: 100 Letters to his Agents in London and Italy* (privately printed, 1982), p. 124.

20   Brian Reade and Elizabeth Glass, 'Notes on Christie's from 1766 to 1945, compiled from sales catalogues of Messrs. Christie, Manson and Wood' (National Art Library, 1949). Their criteria for selection are broad, including architects and collectors. It has also been calculated that Christie's handled two-thirds of the artists' studio sales in and around London between 1770 and 1839. Thomas M. Bayer and John R. Page, *The Development of the Art Market in England: Money as Muse, 1730–1900* (London, 2011), p. 145.

21   *The Yale Edition of Horace Walpole's Correspondence*, ed. W. S. Lewis (New Haven, 1937–83) vol. 32, pp. 279–80: Walpole to Lady Ossory, 4 December 1775.

22   Iain Pears, *The Discovery of Painting: The Growth of Interest in the Arts in England 1680–1768* (New Haven and London, 1988), pp. 208–09.

23   The Poussin was bought from the family by the National Gallery in 1947.

24   Now in the Sterling and Francine Clark Institute, Williamstown, Massachusetts, having been acquired from the last Earl of Chesterfield in 1917. See *Walpole Correspondence*, vol. 32, pp. 102–03: Walpole to Lady Ossory, 11 March 1773 and vol. 23, p. 466: Walpole to Horace Mann, 12 March 1773. According to Fanny Burney, Chesterfield was so ill that Christie sent the pictures to his room for him to examine them. He died eighteen days later. *Early Diary of*

*Frances Burney*, ed. A R. Ellis (London, 1913), vol. 1, p. 205.

25 *Walpole Correspondence*, vol. 23, p. 569: Walpole to Horace Mann. The merchant banker Sir George Colebrooke (1729–1829) speculated unsuccessfully in hemp and failed to corner the market in alum. His family bank closed on 31 March 1773; ninety-four pictures were sold by Christie's on 22–23 April 1774 for £4,385 15s, and his library and print collection was sold in 1777, the year of his bankruptcy.

26 Dries Lyna, 'In Search of a British Connection: Flemish Dealers on the London Art Market and the Taste for Continental Painting (1750–1800)', in Charlotte Gould and Sophie Mesplàde eds., *Marketing Art in the British Isles, 1700 to the Present: A Cultural History* (Farnham, 2012), pp. 101–17. Stephen Benson, *The Life and Work of Benjamin Vandergucht 1752–1794* (London, 2012).

27 For example, the picture collection of Gerard Vandergucht on 6–8 March 1777 and that of his son Benjamin Vandergucht on 11–12 March 1796. Other posthumous trade sales include that of Richard Dalton's picture and sculpture collection on 9–11 April 1791 and John Bertels's from 31 January to 2 February 1793, while the pictures of Walsh Porter 'going abroad' were sold on 22–23 March 1803.

28 Brigstocke 1982 (see note 19), pp. 118–25: Buchanan to David Stewart, 24 January 1804.

29 Brigstocke 1982, p. 3, quoting British Library, Add MS 36497, f. 152.

30 National Art Library, 'Sale catalogues of the principal collections of pictures (one hundred & seventy one in number) sold by auction in England within the years 1711–1759. The greater part of them with the prices & names of purchasers.' This two-volume dealer's record is known as the Houlditch manuscripts. For the Schaub sale see the annotated catalogue in the British Library, 7805.e.5 (6).

31 In the event, this sale did not take place, as his friends rallied round to pay off his most pressing debts.

32 *British Museum Satires VII*, 8888.

33 *British Museum Satires V*, 6101 and *VII*, 8526.

34 Cynthia Wall, 'The English Auction: Narratives of Dismantlings', in *Eighteenth-Century Studies* 31 (1997–98), pp. 1–25. The article fails to allow for the fact that the majority of buyers, then as now, were trade.

35 John Taylor, *Records of My Life* (London, 1832), vol. 2, pp. 206–11.

36 Now in the J. Paul Getty Museum, Los Angeles.

37 This is based on gossip with Harry Philips, Christie's former chief clerk who started his own business in 1796, so not a wholly reliable source. *The Diary of Joseph Farington*, eds. Kenneth Garlick and Angus Macintyre (New Haven

and London, 1978), vol. 3, p. 395: 4 February 1798.

38  Benson 2012 (see note 26), pp. 80–82.

39  *Walpole Correspondence*, vol. 2, pp. 168–70: Walpole to Rev Mr Cole, 12 July
    1779. Andrew Moore, 'The Houghton Sale', in Brian Allen and Larissa Dukel-
    skaya, *British Art Treasures from Russian Imperial Collections in the Hermitage*
    (New Haven and London, 1997), pp. 46–55.

40  Charles-Alexandre de Calonne (1734–1802), appointed controller general of
    finance to Louis XVI in 1783, was an early arrival in London, following his
    dismissal in 1787. W. Buchanan, *Memoirs of Painting, with a chronological histo-
    ry of the emportation of pictures of the great masters into England since the French
    Revolution* (London, 1824), vol. 1, pp. 218–19.

41  Transcripts of letters written from Paris by P. J. Tassaert to James Christie in
    June 1790, Christie's archives. Francis Russell, 'James Christie, P. J. Tassaert
    and the Negotiations for the Orleans Collection', *Christie's International Mag-
    azine* (May 1990), pp. 8–10.

42  Bryan's temporary showroom was just east of Christie's, on the other side of
    Cumberland House. Julia Armstrong-Totten, 'The Rise and Fall of a British
    Connoisseur: The Career of Michael Bryan (1757–1821), Picture Dealer Ex-
    traordinaire', in *Auctions, Agents and Dealers: The Mechanisms of the Art Market
    1660–1830*, ed. Jeremy Warren and Adriana Turpin (Oxford, 2007), pp. 141–50.
    For accounts of the sale, see Buchanan 1824 (see note 40), vol. 1, pp. 9–216.
    Nicholas Penny, *National Gallery Catalogues (new series): The Sixteenth-Century
    Italian Paintings*, vol. 2: *Venice 1540–1600* (London, 2008), pp. 466–70.

43  *Farington Diary* (see note 37), vol. 2, p. 376: 12 August 1795; and vol. 3, p. 792:
    9 March 1797.

44  Buchanan 1824 (see note 40), vol. 1, pp. 257–70.

45  For example, the anonymous sale of works acquired by John Udney, British
    consul in Leghorn, on 25 April 1800, and the first of three sales of the Italian
    paintings that William Young Ottley prized out of Roman patrician families
    in 1798–99, during the French occupation of the city, offered for sale on
    16 May 1801. Buchanan 1824 (see note 40), vol. 2, pp. 11–19 and pp. 20–30.


## 2  Pompeii 1875

46  Manfred Reitz, *Berühmte Kunstsammler* (Frankfurt and Leipzig, 1998),
    p. 76. p. 12.

47  Karl Wilhelm, *Wirtschafts- und Sozialgeschichte des Kunstauktionswesens in
    Deutschland vom 18. Jahrhundert bis 1945* (Munich, 1990), pp. 10ff.

48 Reitz 1998 (see note 46), p. 12.

49 Thurn 1994 (see note 5), p.14; Reitz 1998 (see note 46) pp. 14, 17.

50 Peter Watson, *From Manet to Manhattan: The Rise of the Modern Art Market* (New York, 1992), p. xiii; Thurn 1994 (see note 49), p. 19.

51 Reitz 1998 (see note 46), p. 18.

52 Thurn 1994 (see note 5), pp. 19–20.

53 Gerald Reitlinger, *The Economics of Taste*, vol. II: *The Rise and Fall of Objets d'art Prices Since 1750* (London, 1963), p. 9.

54 See also Gore Verbinski's *Pirates of the Caribbean* film series (from 2003), where auction sales are a regular distribution channel for brides; see also Wilhelm 1990 (see note 47), p. 18.

55 Wilhelm 1990 (see note 47) p. 18.


## 2 Lucius Caecilius Iucundus: Messages from the Art Market in Antiquity

56 See Matthew Sturgis, *When in Rome: 2,000 Years of Roman Sightseeing* (London, 2011); Jason M. Kelly, *The Society of Dilettanti: Archaeology and Identity in the British Enlightenment* (New Haven, 2010).

57 See Thomas Freller, *Adlige auf Tour: Die Erfindung der Bildungsreise* (Ostfildern, 2007); Constanze Baum, 'Vorbild-Abbild-Zerrbild: Bewältigungsstrategien Europäischer Neapelreisender um 1800', in *Dreckige Laken: Die Kehrseite der 'Grand Tour'*, ed. Joseph Imorde and Erik Wegerhoff (Berlin, 2012).

58 Marion Mannsperger, 'Archäologie in den Vesuvstädten: Die Geschichte der Entdeckungen bis zum Beginn der modernen Ausgrabungen', in *Bilder aus Pompeii: Antike aus zweiter Hand*, ed. Marion Mannsperger and Joachim Migl (Ostfildern, 1998), pp. 19–22.

59 The panels were sewn with thread into booklets of two or three tablets each.

60 Theodor Mommsen, 'Die pompejanischen Quittungstafeln des L. Caecilius Jucundus', in *Hermes Zeitschrift für klassische Philologie* 12 (Berlin, 1877), pp. 89, 115.

61 Thurn 1994 (see note 5), pp. 19.

62 Mommsen 1877 (see note 60), with further references.

63 Ibid., pp. 98, 102.

64 A third party, who is excluded from the contract between seller and auctioneer, but who will guarantee a minimum auction sale price to the seller.

65 Jean Andreau, *Banking and Business in the Roman World* (Cambridge, 1999), p. 70; Katherine E. Welch, 'Pompeian Men and Women in Portrait Sculpture', in *The World of Pompeii*, ed. John J. Dobbins and Pedar Foss (New York, 2007), pp. 42.

66  Thurn 1994 (see note 5), p. 21.

67  Mommsen, 1877 (see note 60), p. 97.


### 3  London 1882

---

68  Krysztof Pomian, *Der Ursprung des Museums: Vom Sammeln* (Berlin, 1988),
    pp. 69; Hannelore Sachs, *Sammler und Mäzene: Von der Entwicklung des
    Kunstsammelns von der Antike bis zur Gegenwart* (Leipzig, 1971), pp. 140ff.

69  Holger Liebs, 'Die Kunst und das Geld', in *Die Kunst, das Geld und die Krise*
    (Cologne, 2009), p. 27.

70  Wilhelm 1990 (see note 47), p. 42; Walter Grasskamp, *Die unbewältigte
    Moderne: Kunst und Öffentlichkeit* (Munich, 1994), p. 18.

71  Holger Liebs, 'Paradigma und Paragone', in *In Between*, ed. Wilfried Dieck-
    hoff and Kasper König (Cologne, 2000), p. 22.

72  Watson 1992 (see note 50), p. 39; see also chapter four, 'Berlin 1916–1932'
    in ibid.

73  Reitlinger 1961 (see note 7), p. 176.

74  Christian Herchenröder, *Die Kunstmärkte* (Dusseldorf and Vienna, 1978), p. 7.

75  Reitlinger 1963 (see note 53), p. 11.


### 4  Berlin 1916–1932

---

76  Watson 1992 (see note 50), p. 42ff.

77  See Katharina Hegewisch, *Das Ende der Avantgarde: Kunst als Dienstleistung*
    (Munich, 1995).

78  Ambroise Vollard, *Erinnerungen eines Kunsthändlers* (Zurich, 1980), p. 63.

79  Pierre Assouline, *An Artful Life* (New York, 1991), pp. 54ff.

80  Reitlinger 1961 (see note 7), p. 214.

81  Thurn 1994 (see note 5), p. 126.

82  Reitlinger 1963 (see note 53), pp. 5, 9.

83  Reitlinger 1961 (see note 7), pp. 207ff.

84 Stephanie Barron, '1937: Moderne Kunst und Politik im Vorkriegsdeutsch-
land', in Stephanie Barron and Peter Guenther, *Entartete Kunst! Das Schicksal
der Avantgarde im Nazi-Deutschland*, exh. cat. Los Angeles County Museum
of Art and Deutsches Historisches Museum, Berlin (Munich, 1992), p. 9.
Also published as *Degenerate Art: The Fate of the Avant-garde in Nazi Germany*
(Los Angeles, 1991).

85 Lynn Nicholas, *Der Raub der Europa* (Munich 1997), p. 17ff. Originally published as *The Rape of Europa: The Fate of Europe's Treasures in the Third Reich and
the Second World War* (New York, 1994).

86 Thurn 1994 (see note 5), p. 169.

87 Jonathan Petroloulos, *Kunstraub und Sammelwahn* (Berlin, 1999), pp. 121–22.

88 Matthias Frehner, '"Das wird toll und immer toller": Der größte Kunstraub
der Geschichte', in *Das Geschäft mit der Raubkunst*, ed. Matthias Frehner
(Zurich, 1998), p. 83; Konstantin Akisha und Grigorii Kozlov, *Beautiful Loot:
The Soviet Plunder of Europe's Art Treasures* (New York, 1995), pp. 43, 72; Natalia
Volkert, *Kunst- und Kulturraub im Zweiten Weltkrieg* (Frankfurt am Main,
2000), pp. 63ff.

89 Nicholas 1997 (see note 85), pp. 207–08; Hector Feliciano, *Das verlorene
Museum* (Berlin, 1998), pp. 127–28.

90 Feliciano 1998 (see note 89), pp. 152–53.

91 Esther Francini, Georg Kreis and Anja Heuss, *Fluchtgut – Raubgut: Der
Transfer von Kulturgütern in und über die Schweiz 1933–1945 und die Frage der
Restitution* (Zurich, 2001).




92 Galerie Fischer, *Gemälde und Plastiken aus moderner Meister aus deutschen Mu-
seen* (Lucerne, 30 June 1939). See Stephanie Barron, 'Die Auktion in der Galerie Fischer', in Barron and Guenther 1992 (see note 84), pp. 135–169; Stefan
Frey, 'Die Auktion der Galerie Fischer in Luzern am 30. Juni 1939: ein Aus-
verkauf der Moderne aus Deutschland?' in *Überbrückt: Ästhetische Moderne
und Nationalsozialismus; Kunsthistoriker und Künstler 1925–1937*, ed. Eugen
Blume and Dieter Scholz (Cologne, 1999), pp. 275–89; Gesa Jeuthe, 'Die Moderne unter dem Hammer: Zur "Verwertung" der "entarteten" Kunst durch die
Luzerner Galerie Fischer 1939', in *Angriff auf die Avantgarde: Kunst und Kunst-
politik im Nationalsozialismus*, ed. Uwe Fleckner (Berlin, 2007), pp. 189–267.

93  For an analysis of the sale results see Jeuthe 2007 (see note 92).

94  Ibid.

95  Concerning the role Fischer played, see Barron 1992 (see note 84), Jeuthe 2007 (see note 92); Also Francini, Heuss, and Kreis 2001 (see note 91), pp. 280–309 and 373–412; for 'emigrant auctions', see pp. 156–64.

96  See Christine Fischer-Defoy's contribution to *Gute Geschäfte: Kunsthandel in Berlin 1933–45*, ed. Christine Fischer-Defoy and Kaspar Nürnberg, exh. cat. Centrum Judaicum, Berlin and Landesarchiv Berlin (Berlin, 2011), p. 10. See also Angelika Enderlein, *Der Berliner Kunsthandel in der Weimarer Republik und im NS-Staat: Zum Schicksal der Sammlung Graetz* (Berlin, 2006).

97  Anja Heuss, 'Die Reichskulturkammer und die Steuerung des Kunsthandels in Dritten Reich', in *sediment: Mitteilungen zur Geschichte des Kunsthandels* 3 (1998), pp. 49–61.

98  See Angelika Enderlein's contribution to exh. cat. *Gute Geschäfte* 2011 (see note 96) p. 137.

99  See Patrick Golenia's contribution to exh. cat. *Gute Geschäfte* 2011 (see note 96), pp. 20–21.

100  Enderlein in exh. cat. *Gute Geschäfte* 2011 (see note 96), p. 138; also Heuss 1998 (see note 97).

101  This is demonstrated in Meike Hoppe's study of the Weinmüller auction house in Munich: Meike Hopp, *Kunsthandel im Nationalsozialismus: Adolf Weinmüller in München und Wien* (Cologne et al., 2012).

102  See Kaspar Nürnberg's contribution to exh. cat. *Gute Geschäfte* 2011 (see note 96), p. 111.

103  The *Verordnung gegen die Unterstützung Tarnung jüdischer Gewerbebetriebe* was issued on April 22, 1938.


## 6  Stuttgart 1947–1962

104  Thurn 1994 (see note 5), p. 210.

105  Roman Norbert Ketterer, *Dialoge: Stuttgarter Kunstkabinett und Moderne Kunst* (Stuttgart and Zurich, 1988), pp. 206ff.

106  Christian Herchenröder, *Die Kunstmärkte im Wandel* (Dusseldorf, 2000), p. 21.

107  Eva Karcher, 'Auf der Suche nach dem Gleichgewicht zwischen Marktelite und Populärkultur', in *Galerien in Deutschland: Schnittstelle Kunst + Markt*, ed. Bernd Fesel and Maximilian Krips (Cologne, 2000), p. 20.

108  Rudolf Scharpff, *Der Mann mit der Postkarte* (Ostfildern-Ruit, 2004), p. 11.

109   Manfred Schneckenburger, *documenta: Idee und Institution* (Munich, 1983), p. 66.

110   Reitlinger 1961 (see note 7), p. 220.

111   'Kunsthandel: Porzellan Auktion; Boettger-Hausse', *Der Spiegel* 29 (July 13, 1960), pp. 62–64.

## 6   Roman Norbert Ketterer, or the Return of Expressionism

112   Sybille, *Der Stern* (21 May 1961), quoted in Ketterer 1988 (see note 105), vol. 1, p. 371.

113   Ibid.

114   Julia Friedrich and Andreas Prinzing, eds., *So fing man einfach an, ohne viele Worte: Ausstellungswesen und Sammlungspolitik in den ersten Jahren nach dem Zweiten Weltkrieg*, mus. cat. (Cologne, 2012), p. 59.

115   Ketterer 1988 (see note 105), p. 21.

116   Friedrich and Prinzing 2012 (see note 114), p.13.

117   Ketterer 1988 (see note 105), vol. 1, pp. 27–28.

118   Ibid., vol. 2, p. 318.

119   Ibid., p. 209.

120   Ibid., p. 310

121   Ibid., p. 311.

122   Ketterer 1988 (see note 105), vol. 1, p. 395

123   Ketterer 1988 (see note 105), vol. 2, p. 202

## 7   Bern 1951

124   Frank Herrmann, *Sotheby's: Portrait of an Auction House* (London, 1980), p. 322.

125   Serge Guilbaut, *Wie New York die Idee der modernen Kunst gestohlen hat* (Dresden and Basel, 1997), pp. 71ff.

126   Christian von Faber-Castell, *Koller: 50 Jahre Kunsthandel und Auktionen* (Zurich, 2008), p. 55.

127   Antje-Katrin Uhl, *Der Handel mit Kunstwerken im europäischen Binnenmarkt* (Berlin, 1993), p. 102.

128   Faber-Castell 2008 (see note 126), pp. 33, 81–82.

129   Katja Blomberg, *Wie Kunstwerte entstehen* (Hamburg, 2005), pp. 74–75.

130   Quentin Byrne-Sutton, Fabienne Geisinger-Mariethoz, *Art-Law Guide* (Geneva, 1999), p. 64.

### 8   London 1957–58 and 1977

131   Wendell Garrett, 'The Auction House Revisited', in *Sotheby's: Art at Auction* (London, 1994), p. 55.

132   Watson 1992 (see note 50), pp. 312, 318.

133   John Herbert, *Inside Christie's* (New York, 1990), p. 19.

134   Robert Wraight, *Das Geschäft mit der Kunst* (Munich, 1966), p. 34.

135   Reitlinger 1961 (see note 7), p. 232.

136   Georgina Adam, *Big Bucks: The Explosion of the Art Market in the 21st Century* (Farnham and Burlington, 2014), p. 36.

137   Herchenröder 2000 (see note 106), pp. 11, 14.

138   Herchenröder 2000, p. 10; Harald Siebenmorgen, *Für Baden gerettet* (Karlsruhe, 1996), pp. 13–14.

139   Reitlinger 1963 (see note 53), p. 2.

140   Herchenröder 1978 (see note 74), p. 14.

### 9   Basel 1964

141   John Herbert 1990 (see note 133), pp. 44–44.

142   Lacey 1998 (see note 8), pp. 38ff.; Sarah Thornton, *Seven Days in the Art World* (London, 2008), p. 12.

143   Faber-Castell 2008 (see note 126), p. 76.

### 10   New York 1990

144   Reitlinger 1963 (see note 53), p. 16.

145   According to the list, in November 1989 alone, fifty-eight art works had sold for over five million dollars, 305 for over one million dollars; and in addition works by Pablo Picasso had sold for a total of $377 million. Watson 1992 (see note 50), p. 412.

146   See Cynthia Saltzman, *Das Bildnis des Dr. Gachet: Biographie eines Meisterwerks* (Frankfurt am Main and Leipzig, 2000).

147   Herchenröder 2000 (see note 106), p. 9.

148  Ronald de Leeuw, ed., *The Letters of Vincent van Gogh*, trans. Arnold Pomerans (London and New York, 1997), p. 356.

149  Quoted in Fred Orton and Griselda Pollock, *Vincent van Gogh: Artist of his Time* (New York, 1978), p. 77.

150  On van Gogh's Expressionism, see Philip Hook, *Breakfast at Sotheby's: An A-Z of the Art World* (London, 2013), pp. 157–58. On melancholy, see Nienke Bakker et al. *The Real Van Gogh: The Artist and His Letters* (London, 2010) p. 22.

151  Louis van Tilborgh, *Van Gogh and Japan* (Amsterdam, 2006), pp. 268–71.

152  Bernard Denvir, *The Chronicle of Impressionism: A Timeline History of Impressionist Art* (London New York, 1993), pp. 239, 249.

153  Gregory Irvine, ed. *Japonisme and the rise of the modern art movement: the arts of the Meiji period* (London and New York, 2013), p. 26.

154  Maurice Rheims, *Art on the Market: Thirty-Five Centuries of Collecting and Collectors from Midas to Paul Getty* (London, 1961), p. 169.

155  Irvine 2013 (see note 153), p. 103.

156  James Henry Rubin, *Impressionism* (London, 1999), pp. 73–76, 188–89.

157  Van Tilborgh 2006 (see note 151), p. 10.

158  Denvir 1993 (see note 152), p. 156; Irvine 2013 (see note 153), p. 9.

159  Van Tilborgh 2006 (see note 151), pp. 14–17.

160  Van Tilborgh 2006, p. 40; John Rewald, *Post-Impressionism: from Van Gogh to Gauguin* (1956), third edition (New York, 1979), p. 193.

161  Van Tilborgh 2006 (see note 151), pp. 36–37.

162  Watson 1992 (see note 50), pp. 104–05; pp. 123–24.

163  Reitlinger 1961 (see note 7), p. 330.

164  Vincent van Gogh, *The Letters: Publication History*, Van Gogh Museum, Amsterdam: www.vangoghletters.org/vg/publications_4.html (accessed July 4, 2014).

165  Gerald Reitlinger, *The Economics of Taste*, vol. 3: *The Art Market in the 1960s* (London, 1970), p. 183.

166  Ibid., p. 184.

167  Richard Rush, *Art as an Investment* (Englewood Cliffs, NJ, 1961), p. 38.

168  Reitlinger 1970 (see note 165), p. 182.

169  Naohiro Ogawa et al., 'Rapid Population Aging and Changing Intergenerational Transfers in Japan', in *International Handbook of Population Aging*, ed. Peter Uhlenberg (Berlin, 2009), p. 136.

170  Reitlinger 1963 (see note 53), pp. 222–24.

171  Reitlinger 1970 (see note 165), pp. 558–60.

172 John Parker, *Great Art Sales of the Century* (London, 1975), pp. 73–75.

173 Denvir 1993 (see note 152), pp. 250, 251.

174 Watson 1992 (see note 50), p. 393.

175 Christopher Wood, *The Great Art Boom 1970–97* (Weybridge, Surrey, 1997), p. 111.

176 Watson 1992 (see note 50), p. 386.

177 FxTop, USD/JPY, www.fxtop.com/en/historical-exchange-rates (accessed 4 July 2014).

178 Watson 1992 (see note 50), p. 412.

179 Ibid., p. 414.

180 Ibid., p. 9.

181 James Goodwin, 'Art's Value: Provenance' (lecture), June 2014.

182 Yahoo Finance, 'Nikkei 225 index', https://uk.finance.yahoo.com (accessed 4 July 2014).

183 Watson 1992 (see note 50), p. 24.

184 Ibid., p. 25.

185 Lord Carrington, Foreword to *Christie's Review of the Season 1990*, ed. Anne Montefiore (London, 1991).

186 Merril Stevenson, 'A Survey of the World Art Market', *The Economist* (22 December 1990).

187 Wikipedia, 'List of Most Expensive Paintings', http://en.wikipedia.org/wiki/List_of_most_expensive_paintings (accessed 4 July 2014).

## 11 New York, London, Geneva and Zurich 2000–01

188 Christopher Mason, *The Art of the Steal (New York, 2004), pp. 3ff; A. Alfred Taubman, Threshold Resistance: The Extraordinary Career of a Luxury Retailing Pioneer* (New York, 2007), pp. 161ff.

189 Katja Blomberg, *Wie Kunstwerte entstehen*, Hamburg, 2005, p. 10.

190 Silvia von Bennigsen, Irene Gludowacz, Susanne van Hagen, *Global Art* (Ostfildern, 2009), p. 268.

191 Adam 2014 (see note 136), p. 28.

192 Don Thompson, *The Supermodel and the Brillo Box* (New York, 2014), p. 3.

## 12 Paris 2001–2009

193 Serge Guilbaut, *Wie New York die Idee der modernen Kunst gestohlen hat* (Dresden, Basel, 1997), p. 71.

194   Alden R. Gordon, 'The System Governing Appraised Value in Ancien
      Régime France', in *Auctions, Agents and Dealers: The Mechanisms of the Art
      Market 1660–1830*, ed. Adriana Turpin and Jeremy Warren (Oxford and
      London, 2008).
195   Alexis Fournol and Melanie Gerlis, 'The Slow Decline of the Drouot',
      *The Art Newspaper* (June 2014).
196   See Yann Gaillard, Alain Quemin, Philippe Chalmin, Christian Borel,
      Gerard Sousi, and Laurence Mauger, *Code des ventes volontaires et judicaires*
      (Lyon, 2001).
197   François Duret-Robert, *Ventes d'oeuvres d'art* (Paris, 2001), pp. 87.
198   TEFAF, *The International Art Market 2007–2009* (Maastricht, 2010).

### 13   New York 2004

199   Pierre Bourdieu, *Die feinen Unterschiede: Kritik der gesellschaftlichen Urteilskraft*
      (Frankfurt am Main, 1982), pp. 44ff.; Wolfgang Max Faust and Gerd de Vries,
      *Hunger nach Bildern* (Cologne, 1982), pp. 39ff.
200   Wolfgang Ulrich, *Mit dem Rücken zur Kunst* (Berlin, 2000), pp. 12–13.
201   Christian Herchenröder, *Die neuen Kunstmärkte* (Dusseldorf, 1990), p. 40.
202   Herchenröder 2000 (see note 106), p. 189; Don Thompson, *The $12 Million
      Stuffed Shark: The Curious Economics of Contemporary Art* (London, 2008), p. 174.
203   Piroschka Dossi, *Hype! Kunst und Geld* (Munich, 2007), pp. 36ff.; Thompson
      2008 (see note 202), pp. 173ff.
204   Adam 2014 (see note 136), p. 17.
205   Matthew Collings, *Art Crazy Nation* (London, 2001), pp. 84ff.; Charles
      Saatchi, *My Name is Charles Saatchi and I am an Artoholic* (London, 2009),
      pp. 82–83; Gregor Muir, *Lucky Kunst: The Rise and Fall of Young British Art*
      (London, 2009), pp. 200–01.
206   TEFAF, *The International Art Market in 2006* (Maastricht, 2007).
207   Katja Blomberg, *Wie Kunstwerke entstehen* (Hamburg, 2005), p. 10;
      Adam 2014 (see note 136), p. 34, 133.
208   Liebs 2009 (see note 69), p. 31.
209   Thompson 2014 (see note 192), pp. 2, 4.

### 14   New York 2013

210   Isabelle Graw, *Der große Preis: Kunst zwischen Markt und Celebrity Kultur*

(Cologne, 2008), pp. 113ff., 142ff; Thompson 2014 (see note 192), pp. 28, 73–74; Michael Findlay, *The Value of Art* (Munich et al. 2014), p. 152.

211 Georgina Adam, *Big Bucks: The Explosion of the Art Market in the 21st Century* (Farnham and Burlington, 2014), p. 10.

212 TEFAF, *Art Market Report 2014* (Maastricht 2014); Thompson 2014, p. 24.

213 Adam 2014 (see note 136), p. 9.

214 Thompson 2008 (see note 202), pp. 175–76; Silvia von Bennigsen, Irene Gludowacz, and Susanne von Hagen, *Global Art* (Ostfildern, 2009), p. 268; Adam 2014 (see note 136), p. 40.

## 15 The Day-to-day Business of Auctioneering

215 There are of course general regulations for the sale of goods.

216 In Germany and Switzerland this can in some instances even transfer legal title on objects that have been stolen, misappropriated or lost.

217 Ketterer 1988 (see note 105), pp. 151–52. See chapter 6.

218 Christian Herchenröder, *Auktionen* (Zurich, 2003), pp. 72–73.

219 Ibid., p. 53.

220 Christian Heath, *The Dynamics of Auction* (New York, 2013), pp. 88, 94–95.

221 Thornton 2008 (see note 142), p. 8.

222 Watson 1992 (see note 50), pp. 22–23; Heath 2013 (see note 220), pp. 89–90.

223 Lacey 1998 (see note 142), p. 341.

224 Wilhelm 1990 (see note 47), p. 82.

225 Thornton 2008 (see note 142), p. 10.

226 Wraight 1966 (see note 134), p. 64; Richard Engelbrecht-Wiggans, 'An Introduction to the Theory of Bidding for a Single Object', in *Auctions, Bidding, and Contracting*, ed. Engelbrecht-Wiggans, Martin Schubik et al. (New York, 1983), p. 133.

227 Thompson 2008 (see note 202), p. 8.

228 Ketterer 1988 (see note 105), p. 169.

229 Herchenröder 2003 (see note 218), p. 56.

230 Watson 1992 (see note 50), pp. 11, 22.

## 17 A Bid for Love: *The Heir* by Vita Sackville-West

231 Martin Suter, *Der letzte Weynfeldt* (Zurich, 2008).

232 Peter Watson, *Crusade* (London, 1987).

# Appropriation List
# Auctioneering in Books, Movies, and Popular Culture

## Books

Bongartz, Barbara. *Die Schönen und die Reichen*. Frankfurt am Main, 2011.

Bongartz, Barbara. *Perlensamt*. Frankfurt am Main,  2009.

Fernyhough, Charles. *The Auctioneer*. London, 1999

Grossberg, Benjamin J. *The Auctioneer Bangs His Gavel* (poetry chapbook). Kent, OH, 2006

Nilsen, Anna. *Art Auction Mystery: Find the Fakes, Save the Sale!* (for children aged 10 and up). Boston, 2005

Martin, Steve. *An Object of Beauty: A Novel*. New York, 2010

Sackville-West, Vita. *The Heir*. London 1922.

Samson, Joan. *The Auctioneer*. London, 1976

Serrell, Philip. *An Auctioneer's Lot: Tales from a Country Auctioneer*. London, 2006

Serrell, Philip. *Sold to the Man with the Tin Leg*. London, 2007

Shapton, Leanne. *Important Artifacts and Personal Property from the Collection of Lenore Doolan and Harold Morris, Including Books, Street Fashion, and Jewelry*. New York, 2009.

Suter, Martin. *Der letzte Weynfeldt*. Zurich, 2008

Voilier, Claude. *Les Cinqs se Mettent en Quatre*, Paris, 1975 (continuing the children's series by Enid Blyton). English edition: *The Famous Five and the Pink Pearls*. Translated by Anthea Bell. New York, 1987.

Watson, Peter. *Crusade*. London, 1987

## Games and Characters in Comics

*Auction Wars: Storage King*, by GameDigits Ltd (for iOS), 2013. ("A great new storage auction game that allows you to battle against other buyers, make the right call and walk away rich.")

*Masterpiece: The Art Auction Game*, a board game from Parker Brothers Inc., Salem, Mass., 1970 ("Players compete with other players to bid on potentially valuable paintings and negotiate with other players to trade these works of art, build a portfolio, amass money, and win the game.")

*World of Warcraft* (by Blizzard Entertainment). Auctions feature prominently in this MMORPG (massively multiplayer online role-playing game). Virtual auction houses are available for players to buy and sell items to others. With circa seven million players to date, WOW is the highest grossing video game of all time.

The Auctioneer (and Auctioneer II), little-known enemy of Superman's in the DC Comics universe. First appearance: 2006 ("A gigantic alien that uses advanced technology to collect valuable items and beings to auction to the highest bidder.")

Gadgetzan Auctioneer (by Matt Dixon), a character in the *Hearthstone: Hereos of Warcraft* online strategy card game from Blizzard Entertainment. ("He used to run the black market auction house, but there was just too much violence and he had to move.")


## Music

---

'If I had a Hammer (The Hammer Song).' Written in 1949 by Pete Seeger and Lee
    Hays, since covered by 38 artists, with Simon de Pury the sole auctioneer
    among them (Dinemec Studios, 2009).
'The Auctioneer' (also known as 'The Auctioneer's Song'). Written in 1956 by
    Leroy Van Dyke and recorded by Chuck Miller (1956), among others.
'Tobacco Chant: The Song of the Auctioneer,' featuring tobacco auctioneer Bob
    Cage (n. d.).
'The Auctioneer's Chant: A Closer Look.' Track B1 of the seven-inch-single *Green
    Leaves of Gold*. Compiled by John Maxwell and Peter Lovemore (1986).
'The Auctioneer' (tech house single). Dany Cohiba, 2014.
'Sold (The Grundy County Auction Incident)'. Written by Richard Fagan and Robb
    Royer and recorded in 1995 by John Michael Montgomery.

*The Auctioneer.* Script by Charles Klein, with Arthur Lee. Broadway production by David Belasco, starring David Warfield, 1901.

*The Auctioneer.* Directed by Alfred E. Green, with George Sidney and Marian Nixon, 1927.

*Citizen Kane.* Directed by and starring Orson Welles, 1941

*North by Northwest.* Directed by Alfred Hitchcock, with Cary Grant, James Mason and Eva Maria Saint, 1959.

*How to Steal a Million.* Directed by William Wyler, with Audrey Hepburn, Peter O'Toole and Hugh Griffith, 1966.

*The Magic Christian.* Directed by Joseph Mcgrath, with Ringo Starr, Peter Sellers, John Cleese, Roman Polanski, Raquel Welch, Christopher Lee and Yul Brynner, 1969.

*Conversation Piece.* Directed by Luchino Visconti, with Burt Lancaster, Helmut Berger and Silvana Mangano, 1974.

*James Bond: Octopussy.* Directed by John Glen, with Roger Moore, Louis Jourdan and Maud Adams, 1983.

*Donald Duck: Ducktales* (animated television series). Disney Television Animation. Season 1, episode 25 (December 4, 1987): 'Dr. Jekyll & Mr. McDuck'.

*Money Talks.* Directed by Bratt Ratner, with Charlie Sheen, Chris Tucker, 1997.

*Indecent Proposal.* Directed by Adrian Lyne, with Robert Redford and Demi Moore, 1993 *Groundhog Day.* Directed by Harold Ramis, with Bill Murray and Andie MacDowell.

*The Addams Family.* Directed by Barry Sonnenfeld, with Raul Julia, Angelica Huston and Christina Ricci, 1994.

*The First Wives Club.* Directed by Hugh Wilson, with Bette Midler, Goldie Hawn and Diane Keaton, 1996.

*Mousehunt.* Directed by Gore Verbinski, with Nathan Lane and Christopher Walken, 1997.

*Mickey Blue Eyes.* Directed by Kelly Makin, with Hugh Grant, Jeanne Tripplethorn, James Fox and James Caan, 1999.

*Futurama* (US television series since 1999), episode 6: 'A Fishful of Dollars', 2000

*Die Pfefferkörner* (German television series since 1999), episode 25: *Der Silberne Elefant,* 2001.

*Le Divorce.* Directed by by James Ivory, with Kate Hudson and Naomi Watts, 2003.

*Miss Potter.* Directed by Chris Noonan, with Renée Zellweger, Ewan McGregor, 2006.

*Sex and the City* (film). Directed by Michael Patrick King, with Sarah Jessica
    Parker, 2008.
*Sherlock Holmes: A Game of Shadows.* Directed by Guy Ritchie, with Robert
    Downey Jr. and Jude Law, 2011.
*Dracula* (British television series since 2013), episode 7: 'The Dresden Triptych'.
*Trance.* Directed by Danny Boyle, with James McAvoy and Vincent Cassel, 2013.
*The Best Offer.* Directed by Giuseppe Tornatore, with Geoffrey Rush and Donald
    Sutherland, 2013.


## Fine Art and Design

Cherbuin, Daniel: *Moronica*, 2013
Jankowsky, Christian: *Strip the Auctioneer!*, 2010
Pestana, Mariana and Designersblock: *The Auction Room*, London 2011
Siegel, Amie: *Provenance*, 2013
Siegel, Amie: *Lot 248*, 2013


## Restaurants and Pubs

The Auctioneer Restaurant, Brighouse (West Yorkshire)
The Auctioneer, Blackpool (Lancashire)
The Auctioneer, Carlisle (Cumbria)
The Auctioneer, Greenich (London)
The Old Auctioneer, Banbury (Oxfordshire)
The Auctioneers Bar & Diner, Glasgow

# About the Contributors

## Ursula Bode

is an arts journalist, art critic, and editor and lives in Essen and Berlin. She has been a long-term contributor to the feuilleton sections of the *Hannoversche Allgemeine Zeitung, Die Zeit*, and *Süddeutsche Zeitung;* her articles have been published in magazines such as *Architektur & Wohnen*. She also worked for the arts departments of the broadcasting stations NDR and WDR. From 1997 to 2010 she was on the panel of the TV broadcaster 3sat's 'Bilderstreit' programme. She has worked for art foundations and written numerous articles for German museum exhibition catalogues.

## Dirk Boll

studied law in Göttingen and Freiburg im Breisgau and completed his PhD on the framework conditions for the art markets. He began his career at Christie's in London in 1998. After serving as regional representative in Stuttgart in 2000, he became managing director of the company's Swiss subsidiary based in Zurich. Since 2011 he has been back in London as Christie's Managing Director Continental Europe. He holds a professorship for arts management in Hamburg and regularly publishes in international magazines and newspapers on current developments in the art market.

## Barbara Bongartz

is a writer. She has lived in Berlin and currently in Algiers. Her last novels were *Die Schönen und die Reichen,* 2011, and *Perlensamt,* 2009, with the themes of looted art and auctions. www.barbarabongartz.de

## This Brunner

has over forty years of experience in the film industry in Switzerland and abroad.
He is a member of the European Film Academy and the Swiss Film Academy and
is a well-informed observer of the world cinema and the international film festival scene. He has been the curator of Art Basel's Film sector since 1992 and film
curator for Art Basel in Miami Beach since 2002.

## Walter Feilchenfeldt

started to work at Sotheby's London in the Impressionist department in 1965
before joining his family's firm of art dealers. He is considered an expert on Paul
Cézanne and Vincent van Gogh and has contributed to their respective catalogues raisonnés. In 2005 he published his book *By appointment Only: Schriften zu
Kunst und Kunsthandel,* which was also published in English in 2006. He has been
co-curator of exhibitions on Cézanne, Van Gogh and Edgar Degas.

## Celina Fox

trained as a historian at Cambridge, Harvard and Oxford. She was keeper of art
collections at the Museum of London and organised the 'Metropole London/
London World City 1800–1840' exhibition staged at the Kulturstiftung Ruhr,
Villa Hügel, Essen in 1992. She has served as a member of the Heritage Lottery
Fund's expert panel for museums and as vice chair of English Heritage's Blue
Plaque Panel. She has worked on museum developments in Russia and Germany
and written for many publications. Her latest book, *The Arts of Industry in the Age
of Enlightenment,* was published in 2010 by Yale University Press in association
with the Paul Mellon Centre for Studies in British Art.

## James Goodwin

directs the art market courses at Christie's Education in the UK; at Maastricht University in The Netherlands; and at HEC Paris and EuroMed Management in France. He is a visiting lecturer at several European universities as well as in Beijing. His research and writing have appeared in *The Economist*, the *Financial Times* and the *Wall Street Journal* and he has appeared on BBC TV and Radio and on CNN. His book *The International Art Markets: The Essential Guide for Collectors and Investors* was published in 2008.

## Rose-Maria Gropp

studied at the faculty for humanities in Freiburg im Breisgau, where she also completed her doctorate. She was a postgraduate student at the first German Research Training Group for 'Forms of Communication as Forms of Living' at the university of Siegen. At the *Frankfurter Allgemeine Zeitung / Frankfurter Allgemeine Sonntagszeitung* she is responsible for the section of the newspaper that covers the art market.

## Albert Kriemler

is a designer based in St Gallen in Switzerland. He and his brother Peter Kriemler head the fashion house Akris, which was founded by their grandmother. He has shown his collections, which are often inspired by art and architecture, in Paris since 2005.

## Daniella Luxembourg

studied at the Hebrew University, Jerusalem from 1970 to 1975 and was a founding member of the Diaspora Museum in Tel Aviv. In 1984, she co-founded the Sotheby's office in Israel, and later became deputy director of Sotheby's Switzerland. In 1997, she and Simon de Pury founded an art dealership, which later became an auction house. She left the firm in 2004 to work as an independent art advisor and dealer in London and New York.

## David Nash

joined Sotheby's at the age of nineteen in 1961 when the Impressionist department consisted of just two people. Beginning in 1963 he built up the firm's Impressionist team in the US from scratch. After twenty-two years he and his wife
Lucy Mitchell-Innes founded the gallery Mitchell-Innes & Nash, which shows
emerging and established artists in a renowned exhibition program.


## Christopher Maxwell

studied art history in Cambridge in 2001 and London. In 2005 he joined the
Victoria and Albert Museum as an assistant curator in the ceramics and glass sec-
tion, where he specialised in French porcelain. In 2010, he became a curator at the
Royal Collection, with particular responsibility for BBC Radio 4's 'The Art of
Monarchy' series. At the same time he embarked on a PhD at the University of
Glasgow, researching the dispersal of the Hamilton Palace art collection.


## Amie Siegel

is an American artist working with photographs, video, film installations, and
feature films for the cinema. Her work has been exhibited in solo and group exhibitions in the US, Israel and Germany. Her videos and feature films have been
shown widely, including at the film festivals of Cannes, Berlin and New York. In
2010 she received the Boston Institute for Contemporary Art's 2010 Foster Prize
and in 2012 the Sundance Institute Film Fund award.


## Stephanie Tasch

studied art history and wrote her dissertation on Anthony van Dyck. In 1999 she
became a provenance researcher at Christie's. Since 2012 she has worked at the
German Kulturstiftung der Länder (Cultural foundation of the federal states) as
head of acquisition support for art and cultural artefacts 1600–1900, as well as for
literature and publications (Arsprototo/Patrimonia). She lectures on provenance
research at the Freie Universität Berlin and is a member of the Taskforce
Schwabinger Kunstfund.

## Judd Tully

is editor-at-large of *Art + Auction* magazine and a widely published journalist and art critic for a range of publications with a particular interest in the art market, a beat he began to cover in the mid 1980s for the *Washington Post.*


## Brigitte Ulmer

studied history, journalism and political science at the University of Zurich and art history at the Goldsmith College in London. She lives in Zurich. As an arts journalist she contributes articles on art and the art market to the *Neue Zürcher Zeitung, NZZ am Sonntag* and *Bilanz* as well to as other publications and catalogues. She was co-curator of the retrospective exhibition 'Manon: Eine Person at the Helmshaus in Zurich' (2008) and co-editor of the accompanying exhibition catalogue.


## Wolfgang Wittrock

began his career in the art market working for Thomas Borgmann in Cologne. In 1972–73 he did an internship at Galerie Kornfeld in Bern. In 1974 he opened his own business specializing in prints and works on paper, later focusing on the work of Ernst Ludwig Kirchner, Max Beckmann, and Paul Klee. In 2001 he closed his gallery and moved to Berlin, where he continues to work as an advisor and intermediary. In 2012 he purchased the Schweiger archive on the German art trade from 1900 to 1950 with a view to research and publication.

# Acknowledgements

I am enormously grateful to all the authors. My warmest thanks to those others who contributed to this book:

Laure Camboulives
Daniel Cherubin
Melanie Doderer-Winkler
Hugh Edmeades
Alexander Farenholtz
Kuno Fischer
Benedetta Ghione
Wolfgang Henze and
Ingeborg Henze-Ketterer
Erika Jakubovits
Christian Jankowski
Lynda McLeod
Susanne Meyer-Abich
Jutta Nixdorf
Birgid Seynsche-Vautz
Christine Stauffer
Arno Verkade
Christoph Vogtherr
Jan Wilkinson-Brown

# Photo Credits

# Auctioneers Who Made Art History

Editor
Dirk Boll

Copy editor
Miranda Robbins

Translations
Susanne Meyer-Abich

Graphic design and typesetting
Andreas Platzgummer, Hatje Cantz

Typeface
The Sans, Proforma

Production
Heidrun Zimmermann, Hatje Cantz

Reproductions:
Weyhing digital, Ostfildern

Printing and binding
CPI – Clausen & Bosse, Leck

Paper
Maxi Offset 120 g/m²



Published by
Hatje Cantz Verlag
Zeppelinstrasse 32
73760 Ostfildern
Germany
Tel. +49 711 4405-200
Fax +49 711 4405-220
www.hatjecantz.com
A Ganske Publishing Group company

Hatje Cantz books are available
internationally at selected bookstores.
For more information about our
distribution partners, please visit
our website at www.hatjecantz.com.

ISBN 978-3-7757-3903-0 (English)
ISBN 978-3-7757-3902-3 (German)

This book is also available
as an e-book:
ISBN 978-3-7757-3913-9 (English)
ISBN 978-3-7757-3912-2 (German)

Printed in Germany